QUICK TEAM-BUILDING ACTIVITIES FOR BUSY MANAGERS

QUICK
TEAM-BUILDING
ACTIVITIES
FOR
BUSY MANAGERS

50 Exercises That Get
Results in Just 15 Minutes

BRIAN COLE MILLER

⊿AMACOM

AMERICAN MANAGEMENT ASSOCIATION
New York | Atlanta | Brussels | Chicago | Mexico City | San Francisco
Shanghai | Tokyo | Toronto | Washington, D. C.

Special discounts on bulk quantities of AMACOM books are available to corporations, professional associations, and other organizations. For details, contact Special Sales Department, AMACOM, a division of American Management Association, 1601 Broadway, New York, NY 10019.
Tel.: 212-903-8316. Fax: 212-903-8083.
Web site: www.amacombooks.org

This publication is designed to provide accurate and authoritative information in regard to the subject matter covered. It is sold with the understanding that the publisher is not engaged in rendering legal, accounting, or other professional service. If legal advice or other expert assistance is required, the services of a competent professional person should be sought.

Library of Congress Cataloging-in-Publication Data

Miller, Brian Cole, 1956–

Quick teambuilding activities for busy managers : 50 exercises that get results in just 15 minutes / Brian Cole Miller.

p. cm.

Includes index.

ISBN-10: 0-8144-7201-X

ISBN-13: 978-0-8144-7201-9

1. Teams in the workplace—Training of.   2.nGroup relations training.   3. Communication in organizations. Problems, exercises, etc.   4. Interpersonal communication. Problems, exercises, etc.   5.nGroup games.   I. Title. Planning successful meetings and events / Ann J. Boehme.

HD66 .M544   2004

658.4/02 21   2003011316

Printing number

20 19 18 17

CONTENTS

ACKNOWLEDGMENTS

While working with one of my favorite clients in Maine, I ran into two busy managers within minutes of each other. They had similar requests of me. "Brian, can you give me a quick team-building activity? I want to do something to help my staff come together as a team, but we don't have a lot of time. Nothing 'touchy-feely.' Also, nothing that requires any materials or preparation, because I'm late for that staff meeting already!"

From those conversations came the idea for this book.

My thanks to the following busy managers and professionals who made time to help me pull this book together: Bill Weirsma, Wendy Shaw, Dawn Snyder, Gary Siegerst, Brenda Rowe, Alex Rodriguez, Eileen Nunley, Dean Miller, Chris Lowe, Leslie Lampert, Lynn Jackson, Mark Hansen, Daina Gold, Kay Doucette, Joe Davey, Rick Damato, Sara Cope, Mylo Cope, Gail Cope, Caroline Cofer, Ed Buns, and Sarah Beaulieu.

The sources of these activities are numerous. I designed many myself. I modified others from existing games and activities. The rest I learned from others in the field, sometimes as I participated at conferences and seminars. I apologize in advance to anyone I may have not credited for their activities.

Thank you Kiki, Margie, Rudy, Suzanne, Michael, and Jane for teaching me what teamwork is all about.

Thank you Paul Montgomery for the fantastic illustrations.

Biggest thank you to my family—Benjamin, Heidee, Logan, Stacee, Mom-in-law, and especially Tim—for their unbridled support and enthusiasm.

QUICK TEAM-BUILDING ACTIVITIES FOR BUSY MANAGERS

INTRODUCTION

This book is written for the busy manager who wants to add an element of team-building to a meeting. Here is what you can expect:

Every activity takes less than 15 minutes. Busy managers (and their staffs) do not have hours and hours to spend working on their team. They need activities that are quick and to the point. Each activity in this book will take less than 15 minutes to conduct and discuss.

Can you really get results in less than 15 minutes? Yes, as long as your expectations are realistic. Longstanding issues will not be resolved. Age-old antagonists will not emerge as best friends. Major obstacles will not disappear. However, important team issues will be brought to light. Strangers will become acquaintances. Group norms will be established. Feelings will be validated. Camaraderie will be enhanced. In the end, a stronger team spirit will be fostered.

All activities can be done with only a few materials, or even none at all. You will not have to run to the store for odd materials to conduct these activities. In fact, more than half of the activities require nothing more than pen and paper! The materials required for the rest of them are simple things often found at work, such as paper clips, markers, index cards, pennies, old magazines, and so forth. Only a few activities require special materials such as a deck of cards, balloons, or a puzzle.

Each activity has one or more specific, focused objectives. Team-building activities are usually fun, and the ones in this book definitely are. Fun is not the primary focus of any activity in this book, though. Each activity is designed to help your group come together as a team in one way or another. You can have fun while you learn and grow together!

A busy manager like you can run every activity here easily. They are simple to understand and easy to prepare for. Some of them can be conducted successfully moments after you read them for the first time. You can pick up this book on your way to a meeting and use an activity from it right then and there!

The outline for each activity is easy to follow. Each one is presented in the same easy-to-read, bulleted format:

This is . . . explains very briefly what the activity is.

The purpose is . . . tells what the purpose or objective of the activity is.

Use this when . . . gives you clues you should look for that will tell you if this is the right activity for the purpose you and your team are thinking about.

Materials you'll need . . . tells you everything you will need for the activity. Often, it's nothing!

Here's how . . . outlines, step by step, how to conduct the activity.

For example . . . illustrates how the activity may play out, so you get a good sense of what to expect on each one.

Ask these questions . . . lists the best questions for each activity. These are used for the Debrief, the most important part of any team-building activity. During this session, participants discuss what they learned from the activity and relate it to their behavior back on the job.

Tips for success . . . includes things that will help you run you activity more effectively.

Try these variations . . . offers variations on the activity that can be used to spice it up, slow it down, add a level of competition, or otherwise alter it for a slightly different learning experience.

Relax, you will not find any of these types of activities here:

NO "fish bowl" activities in which only a few participants are actively involved while everyone else watches and critiques them.

NO role-plays where participants are given a fictitious role to act out or pretend.

NO demonstrations in which the leader makes a point by demonstrating something while all the participants merely watch and then discuss.

NO outdoor activities requiring large areas, nice weather, and physically fit participants.

NO handouts to prepare, copy, or distribute.

NO "touchy-feely" activities in which participants have to touch each other a lot or share intimate thoughts and feelings, activities that push the manager into the role of psychologist rather than activity leader.

Before we get to the activities, there are two chapters that will help you with *any* team-building activity you want to do.

The first chapter gives you start-to-finish instructions on how to run an effective team-building activity. We will discuss all three phases of the experience: before, during, and after the activity.

Before the activity, you will learn how to decide which activity is best for you and your team. Why pick *any* activity when you can choose one designed specifically for your team's needs? Then learn how to plan and prepare for your activity (even if you have only 2 minutes in the elevator to do so!).

During the activity, you will learn how to set the activity up for success—giving clear instructions, getting your participants to want to take part in it, and making sure they know what to do and how to do it. Then learn what you should do while they are engaged. Finally, you will learn how to conduct the most important element of your activity: the Debrief. This is when your participants connect what they did in the activity with their behavior on the job. If you skip this step, you may as well not even have performed the activity!

After the activity, you will learn how to make the things learned during the activity come alive in the workplace and make sure you and your team truly benefit from having done the activity in the first place.

Then, in the next chapter, we will look at what could go wrong in an activity. Murphy's law dictates that you will eventually hit a bump or two, but that does not mean you have to fail!

The format for each potential problem is the same:

What if . . . describes the potential problem or concern you may face.

What you'll see . . . indicates what you will actually see and hear that tell you this problem has come up.

The most likely causes . . . identifies what usually causes such a problem. Only when you know the cause can you take meaningful action to avoid the problem altogether or deal with it more effectively.

How to prevent this from happening . . . gives ideas on how you can avoid the problem happening in the first place.

What to do if it happens anyway . . . offers suggestions on how to handle the problem if it actually does happen (despite your best preventive efforts!).

Team-building with your staff can be fun, rewarding, and productive. Seeing those creative sparks as your staff learns something important can be very exciting. Stick with it, be patient, and you will see great results after even just a few activities!

PART ONE
GETTING READY

CHAPTER 1

How to Run a Successful Team-Building Activity

Step 1. Before: Select an activity that's good for your team.

The best team-building *activity* can become the worst team-building *experience* when there is no clear objective. Why spend the time, effort, and money on an activity if you can't identify the business reason or team benefit you expect as a result? If all you want is to have some fun and kill some time, play a parlor game and enjoy. But if you want to improve your team's effectiveness, you need to select an activity that will give you your desired results!

Start with a clear objective in mind. What, specifically, do you want your team to learn or accomplish? Think about it. Your goal should be:

- ➤ Attainable by your team.
- ➤ Relevant and applicable to where they are as a team right now.
- ➤ Something that will be reinforced long after this activity.

Plan on this activity being one of many small steps your team will start taking now. Remember, an effective team is built primarily on trust. Trust, and thus team-building, can rarely be accomplished in one giant leap.

Match your goal to the activity in this book that will best help you get the results you want. If there is more than one good match, do one activity now and another one at a later date.

A NOTE ON COMPETITION: Competition can be a good thing. It can excite, energize, and challenge people to participate better. Do not assume that competition naturally brings out the best in everyone, though. It can also deflate, discourage, and create unnecessary lingering conflict. As the final judge in competitive activities, you risk becoming "the bad guy" as well. So only you can say how competitive you want your team-building activity to be. The most important thing is to be deliberate in your decision, so you can justify it with a clear objective if necessary. Consider:

> ➤ The current level of competition within the team.
> ➤ The emotional health of the participants in dealing with defeat.
> ➤ How intimidating or intimidated the participants are.
> ➤ Your ability to diffuse real conflict among the team members.

Step 2. Before: Prepare for your team-building activity.

You want to make sure you are ready for everyone to have a great learning experience. Fifteen minutes of planning and preparation ahead of time may not guarantee success, but it will certainly help you prevent disaster. Your activity will be most effective if you go into it feeling competent and confident.

Read through the entire activity several times. Make sure you are clear on what is to happen and when, why, and how. Visualize that activity happening successfully.

Obtain all necessary materials. Check the materials to make sure they will work well for the activity. For example, see that the dates on the pennies are legible, test the markers for any that have dried out, make sure there are no cards missing from the deck, and so forth. Assume nothing! Always have a few extras on hand, just in case.

Practice what you are going to say when you start the activity with your team. The best way to do this is to explain the activity to a friend or colleague. If he or she doesn't understand you, figure out a way to explain things more clearly until he or she does.

If the activity requires you to have a role (card dealer, judge, moderator, etc.), practice your comments or actions. This will help you feel less nervous during the activity. It will also free your mind to focus on more important things (the participants' reactions, the participants' learning, your own observations, etc.) during the activity.

Set up the room. Make sure the tables, chairs, flipcharts, and/or other items are placed so that they contribute to the activity's success. A classroom style row of chairs is usually the least conducive to team-building activities. Better choices include a large circle, a "U" shape, or small table groups (several individuals gathered around each table). Any specific setup information required for an activity is noted within that activity.

If the activity's rules or steps are lengthy, write them ahead of time, and post them on the wall so everyone can see them throughout the activity.

Anticipate potential problems. Visualize the activity with *your* team, in *your* location. Ask yourself what could go wrong. Take action to prevent those problems from occurring and/or plan the corrective actions you can take if they do occur. The most common problems and how to avoid or deal with them are discussed in the next chapter.

Step 3. During: Explain the activity to the team.

A 1-minute introduction can make all the difference in setting your team up for success! People engage better when they know *why* they are doing something. They also participate better when they under-stand all the rules up front, and when they are clear on exactly what is expected of them.

Set the mood. Welcome the team with enthusiasm and optimism. Team-building is fun! Convey this right away. You don't have to be a cheerleader; even a smile or a warm comment will let your team know they are in for a great time.

Explain what the activity is. Give a very brief overview of what you have planned, so the team can start getting interested and excited.

Explain why you are doing this particular activity. Share with the team what you hope to accomplish in the next 15 minutes. The more they see purpose to the activity, the more likely they will participate and learn what you want them to learn. For a few of the activities in this book, however, you would ruin their impact by sharing the objective up front. In those cases, tell them there is an objective that will become clear to them in a few minutes. Make sure that objective is called out during the Debrief (the discussion that is held immediately after the activity).

Explain the activity's rules or steps. Don't be afraid to read from this book, use notes, or even have them posted on the wall. Speak slowly, and pause after each one. Remember, they haven't had time to read and reread the activity like you have. It's usually easier to explain the activity all at once before responding to any questions from the team.

Have the team move through the activity's steps as you explain them. For example, if the first step of an activity is to divide the group into smaller teams, have them actually do that before you tell them the next step.

A NOTE ON TEAM SIZE: Most activities will not be ruined if smaller groups are not exactly the same size. If the correct size is critical, the odd participant or two could be assigned the role of "Observer." The Observer role is to quietly watch the others participate. During the Debrief, the Observer shares his or her unique observations.

A NOTE ON PAIRING UP: When an activity requires the participants to pair up, use your own participation to even things out. Participate if the number is odd; observe if it is even.

Distribute the materials after you've fully explained the activity. Otherwise, you risk people getting distracted by them and missing key points. Distribute the materials before the explanation only if you have found that the materials help people understand things better.

Step 4. During: Check for understanding before beginning.

People often hesitate to ask for help when they are confused. You can clarify misunderstandings with patience and some simple review questions. You can keep competition from getting out of hand by laying down a few ground rules, but they must be agreed upon up front.

Make sure your team understands the activity. Asking *"Do you understand?"* is the least effective way to check this (who wants to answer *"No"* in front of the group?). *"Do you have any questions?"* is a little better. *"What questions do you have?"* is even better.

However, the best way to check their understanding is to ask questions that force the team to review the steps or rules of the activity. For example, *"How many minutes do you have to complete this?"* or *"What happens if one of your balloons pops?"*

When the activity will result in one or more winners, make sure everyone is clear on what criteria will be used to determine who wins. Then, ask a review question such as *"How exactly does someone win?"* If ties need to be broken, explain how that will be done.

Declare up front that you are the final judge on all disagreements about who wins. You don't want the team to argue about who won and lose sight of the real purpose of the activity.

When you are confident everyone understands the activity and is ready to go, ask one last time, *"What remaining questions do you have before we start?"*

Step 5. During: Run the activity.

Letting the team go through the activity, and possibly even fail, may be difficult for you to let happen. Remember, the activity is a low-risk alternative to letting the participants learn from failures on the job! People learn and retain better when they experience lessons, rather than when they just hear them. Sit back, observe, and let your team experience.

Once they begin the activity, see that they are following the steps or rules. You want them to at least get started down the path to success. Hold off on correction for just a moment, though. They may check themselves. If not, gently bring them back to task.

Encourage and support them all. Especially thank anyone who goes first in an activity. Being first is a scary situation for many. It takes courage to go first and risk embarrassment or failure.

Make yourself available to clarify steps or redirect the team. If appropriate, walk around quietly and watch for opportunities to help the team succeed. Be careful not to do their task for them, though.

Throughout the activity, watch for things you will want to bring up later during the Debrief. It is OK to jot down a note or two to remember.

If the activity is timed, watch the clock, and give a "time check" occasionally. For example, *"Time check: you have 2 minutes left."*

Don't stop the activity unless it really runs amuck. Otherwise, let it run its course. There will be plenty of opportunity to comment on lessons learned during the Debrief.

Step 6. During: Debrief the activity.

The Debrief is the most critical part of the team-building activity. It is the time when effective questions will guide the participants to link what they experienced in the activity with their behavior on the job. If this step is skipped or glossed over, most of the impact of the activity will be lost in a matter of days. If you do the Debrief well, the lessons learned during the activity will stay with the team indefinitely.

Ask the questions outlined in this book immediately. For most questions, there is no right or wrong answer. Allow all answers to be OK. Try not to evaluate or critique any answer; just nod and accept each one as you listen to it. The questions for each activity should lead the team to the conclusions you want them to reach without you having to spell it out for them.

It is fine to read the questions from this book or to use notes. Stop talking, silently read the question, look back at the team, and then ask the question. The few seconds of silence while you read are less noticeable and less offensive to the group than if you read the question aloud while looking at it. Also, making eye contact while you ask the question is more likely to result in responses than if you do it the other way.

Another way to ask the questions is to write them on index cards beforehand. Pass the index cards out, and ask the participants to take turns reading the questions and soliciting responses.

Try not to call on anyone by name unless you have to. Be comfortable with the silence. Once you have asked a question, stop talking and slowly count to 10 in your head. The silence may feel like an eternity to you, but it feels just as long to the group. Eventually someone will answer! Remember, they have never heard the question before, so it may take a few seconds to formulate a response.

Watch for heads nodding, smiles, and other indications that they agree with what is being said by others. Not everyone has to respond to every question for the entire group to learn. If you see reactions that suggest disagreement, ask, *"Does anyone disagree?"* or *"What about an opposing view?"* Call on the one disagreeing only as a last resort.

Repeat or quickly summarize each response offered.

If anyone gives an off-the-wall response or one that is just plain wrong, ask the group how they feel about it rather than correcting someone. This technique will keep it "safe" for all participants to continue answering questions without fear of a reprimand from you.

Even if the activity did not go quite as well as planned, most participants probably learned something. No matter what happened, you can always ask if the group has ever seen anything like this happen back on the job. Ask what can be learned from this experience. The answers may include what can be improved for future team-building activities!

Step 7. After: Reinforce the learning back on the job.

With your help, the activity can continue teaching the participants long after it is over. Reminding participants of the activity and keeping the lessons learned alive will extend its impact. Keep your team focused on behaviors that support the kind of team you are trying to build.

Display anything the team created for the activity back in the workplace. Each time they see that sculpture, flipchart, or cardboard structure, they will be reminded of what they did, how it made them feel, and what it taught them.

If any new terms or special words came up during the activity, use them frequently. Like the visual items mentioned above, these words will prompt a recall of what happened and what they learned.

Refer to the activity and the lessons learned often when you are coaching, giving feedback, or conducting staff meetings. Look for examples of people exhibiting good team behavior related to the activity, and call it out for them and others to see.

If the activity was a huge success, you may want to repeat it soon.

Plan follow-up activities that will reinforce, emphasize, and build upon what was learned this time.

Watch for examples of how the participants used what was learned in the activity and got better results. If you can quantify how their actions are benefiting the organization, call it out for them and others as evidence of success.

Ask participants in your next staff meeting to share what impact the activity has had on them. If you are in remote locations, use e-mail, electronic bulletin boards, and so forth to keep the learning alive.

CHAPTER 2

What Could Go Wrong in a Team-Building Activity

The team-building activities in this book are easy to conduct in most situations. They have been used successfully with hundreds of other groups just like yours. Follow the instructions carefully, and you will be successful, too!

If you have never run such activities before, it is natural to be concerned about what could go wrong. Below are the most common fears and problems managers face in running an activity. Channel the energy your concerns generate into positive actions to avoid problems and/or effectively deal with them if they do happen!

What if . . .   One or more people don't want to participate?

What you'll   ➤ Rolling eyes.
see . . .   ➤ Lack of eye contact with you, or other negative
              body language.
          ➤ Negative comments about the activity or team-
              building in general.
          ➤ Direct comments that they do not want to partici-
              pate.
          ➤ Direct refusal to participate.
          ➤ Participants dragging their feet on getting started.

> Suggestions for an alternate activity *("Why don't we just . . .")*.

The most likely causes . . .
> Past team-building exercises that were unpleasant or unproductive.
> Not understanding the purpose or value of the activity.
> Shyness or fear of being embarrassed.
> The activity doesn't sound fun or worthwhile.

How to prevent this from happening . . .
> Be clear about the purpose of the activity when you introduce it to the group.
> Be sure the purpose of the activity is one that is needed or valued by the group.
> Reassure them that everyone will do it (and no one will be singled out and maybe embarrassed).
> If it's an activity that allows this, have the less shy people go first.
> If you expect resistance from a particular individual, privately approach him or her beforehand to gain his or her commitment to participate.

What to do if it happens anyway . . .
> Unless it's critical, don't make a big deal of it; perhaps after witnessing one or two team-building activities, they will become more willing to participate next time.
> Remind them that in order for it to be team-building, everyone must participate; otherwise, the rest of the group won't benefit from the exercise.
> Let the group know someone doesn't want to participate, and allow them to handle it. (Beware, they may apply more pressure than you would, or they may not allow that person to participate at all.)
> Find a way for the person to still be involved— perhaps as Scorekeeper, or Timekeeper, or Observer

(with the expectation that he or she will offer observations after the activity).

What if . . .	They don't understand the directions I am giving?

What you'll see . . .	➤ Confused looks. ➤ Participants asking each other what to do. ➤ Participants not doing what is expected. ➤ Nothing happens when the activity begins. ➤ Lots of questions for clarification.

The most likely causes . . .	➤ Directions were given out of order. ➤ Directions were poorly explained. ➤ Side bar conversations distracted attention. ➤ Directions were given too fast. ➤ Directions were too lengthy and not posted.

How to prevent this from even happening . . .	➤ Read and reread the directions to make sure *you* understand them well. ➤ Practice explaining the activity to others until they readily understand. Use their questions to help you adjust the way you explain it next time. ➤ Pause after each direction to let it sink in. ➤ Speak slowly as you explain the activity. ➤ Repeat what seems like the obvious when you give directions (e.g., *"First I want you to pair up. That means we need everyone in groups of two—find one partner to be with right now."*).

What to do if it happens anyway . . .	➤ Start over. Repeat all the directions, so the difficult ones are put into context. This time, slow down even more. ➤ Ask someone who did understand to help you explain.

> Do not get frustrated (either with yourself or the team). Stay calm and focused. Be patient with yourself and with them until you are successful.
> Read the directions from the book. If you got it from the book, they will also.
> If applicable, demonstrate the activity.

What if . . . Materials break, don't work, or we don't have enough?

What you'll see . . .
> Not enough materials to go around.
> Materials breaking or not functioning as planned.

The most likely causes . . .
> Not planning ahead.
> Underestimating the number of materials needed.
> Wrong materials being used.

How to prevent this from even happening . . .
> Bring more than enough materials for all possible participants; err on the side of too many rather than too few.
> Practice or test the activity with exactly the materials you'll be working with (using the exact timeframe) to make sure they will work the way you expect.

What to do if it happens anyway . . .
> Use spare materials (if you have extras).
> Improvise with other materials, if possible.
> Adjust the rules of the activity, if possible.
> Reschedule the activity for another time.

What if . . . Someone gets overly competitive?

What you'll see . . .
> Taking the activity too seriously.
> Bending the rules, or even cheating.
> Extreme efforts to win or do better than others.

	➤ Overly discussing the activity afterwards, with a focus on strategies and missed opportunities rather than on learning points.
The most likely causes . . .	➤ A naturally competitive environment in the workplace (e.g., a sales force). ➤ Naturally competitive people. ➤ Conflict in the group. ➤ Too much focus on the activity rather than on learning.
How to prevent this from even happening . . .	➤ Focus the group's attention on the activity's purpose and learning goals when introducing it. ➤ For a naturally competitive group, select activities that encourage teamwork or that have less of an element of competition built into them. ➤ Offer a very minimal prize for the winner during the introduction that will not be a lingering reminder (for example, an exactly 3-second round of applause, rather than a candy bar).
What to do if it happens anyway . . .	➤ Focus the Debrief on what happened, why it happened, group dynamics, and so forth, rather than on who won or did better than whom (you may even have to declare, *"Let's take the focus off the activity itself and discuss what we learned from the activity."*). ➤ Discuss the competitiveness that came out, why it came out, and how helpful or destructive it was. Link those things back to the workplace. ➤ If you must, stop the activity in the middle to remind the group of the activity's purpose and learning goals.
What if . . .	Participants don't join the Debrief discussion?

What you'll see . . .	➤ Lack of eye contact with you, especially right after you ask a question.
	➤ Minimal or one-word responses to your questions.
	➤ Shoulders shrugging.
	➤ Silence.
The most likely causes . . .	➤ They didn't understand your question.
	➤ You haven't given them enough time to formulate an answer.
	➤ They fear embarrassment of a "wrong" answer in front of you or their peers.
	➤ They are angry about something (may be unrelated to the activity).
How to prevent this from even happening . . .	➤ Ask questions slowly.
	➤ Don't be afraid to read the questions from the book.
	➤ Pause (silently count to 10) after each question. This pause may feel like an eternity to you, but it will give participants the time they need to consider an appropriate response.
	➤ Unless they are too far off, accept and appreciate all responses. This is an opportunity to appreciate the diverse thinking styles of your team!
What to do if it happens anyway . . .	➤ Reword or restate questions only if the group tells you that they didn't understand the question; otherwise, let them think.
	➤ As a last resort, call on participants by name to respond.
	➤ Explain that the activity is only as valuable as our ability to transfer what we learned from it back to the workplace. We can start doing that by discussing these questions.
	➤ After asking a question, offer your own observation. Then ask what others saw that was similar to or different from what you just shared.

> When you get responses, emphatically thank the first few participants for contributing.

What if . . . Someone dominates the Debrief?

What you'll see . . .
> One person answering most of the questions.
> One person talking excessively.
> Most participants remaining silent.

The most likely causes . . .
> The person wanted to help you (and the team) by offering the answers.
> The person wanted to show that he or she has the correct answers.
> Other participants didn't volunteer answers.
> Other participants are afraid to differ with the dominant person.
> The person was impatient waiting for others to contribute.
> The person doesn't feel like he or she is being heard or taken seriously.
> The person may be dominating the group in day-to-day work, and this is just an extension of those group norms.

How to prevent this from even happening . . .
> After anyone answers a question, ask, "*What do the rest of you think?*" or "*What else?*" as you make eye contact with other participants. This will give the signal that you are looking for more discussion than just one answer per question.
> Repeat or quickly summarize each comment, and then say, "*Great, who else has an observation?*"
> Be comfortable yourself, waiting for others to respond (a few seconds of silence may encourage others to speak).
> If you expect one person to dominate the discussion, consider talking to that person before the

activity and asking him or her to hold back, or encourage others to contribute.

➤ If the person tends to dominate day to day, begin to address that behavior outside the bounds of this activity.

What to do
if it happens
anyway . . .

➤ When asking questions, avoid making eye contact with the dominating individual.

➤ Begin a few questions with, *"OK, for the rest of you, my next question is . . ."*

➤ Call on a few participants for their thoughts.

➤ In an extreme case, ask the person to hold off speaking until others have had a chance to respond.

➤ Ask, *"Who has a different perspective he or she would like to share with us?"*

What if . . .

The Debrief gets out of hand?

What you'll
see . . .

➤ A gripe session.

➤ Arguing or fighting.

➤ Discussion moving off the topic.

➤ Side bar discussions.

The most
likely
causes . . .

➤ Poor questions asked during the Debrief.

➤ Unresolved team issues.

➤ Lost control.

How to
prevent this
from even
happening
. . .

➤ Unless you are a skilled facilitator, don't veer too far from the questions in this book.

➤ Do not host activities in hopes of resolving deep issues in the team.

➤ Ask one or more team members beforehand what kind of reaction they believe the activity will spark in the team.

➤ Avoid questions that will put anyone on the spot.

	➤ Avoid questions that pit someone against someone else.
What to do if it happens anyway . . .	➤ Step in and stop the discussion(s) before more damage is done; ask, *"How does this discussion apply to what we learned from the activity?"*
	➤ Don't try to assign blame or find the cause.
	➤ Refocus the Debrief with specific, targeted questions (use the questions in this book).
	➤ In a severe case, terminate the activity and Debrief altogether. This may be an ideal time to try to identify the issues at play and figure out what activities to use next.
What if . . .	They don't get what I wanted them to get out of the activity?
What you'll see . . .	➤ Incorrect answers during the Debrief.
	➤ No connection of the activity to the workplace.
	➤ Key participant behaviors or actions during the activity go unnoticed.
The most likely causes . . .	➤ The purpose of the activity was not explained well up front.
	➤ The activity was not the best one to bring out the learning you wanted.
	➤ Debrief questions were not handled well.
How to prevent this from even happening . . .	➤ Be sure to explain the purpose of the activity to the team. Get them to buy into the need to engage and learn.
	➤ Be sure you have a clear learning objective and that the activity you choose will achieve that for your team.
	➤ Let the participants answer the Debrief questions rather than spoon-feed the correct responses to them.

- When you get minimal responses to Debrief questions, ask for clarification or elaboration.
- Avoid helping the participants get through the activity. The more you help, the less they experience, and thus the less they learn and grow.

What to do if it happens anyway . . .
- Disclose to the group what lesson you had hoped to teach, and discuss where that lesson was found in the activity.
- Let it go; accept what they did learn, and build upon that.
- If time permits, redo the activity with a renewed focus on the desired objective.

A FINAL NOTE: Remember, your participants want their activity to be successful just as much as you do!

PART TWO
THE ACTIVITIES

CHAPTER 3

Communication: Listening and Influencing

$2 NEGOTIATION

This is . . .	An activity in which participants negotiate with each other for $2.
The purpose is . . .	Participants find creative solutions to simple problems; they see that a majority vote is not always the most effective way to decide.
Use this when . . .	➤ Individuals are focusing too much on their own needs. ➤ Individuals need to practice creativity (in problem solving). ➤ The group relies heavily on "majority rules" for making decisions.
Materials you'll need . . .	➤ Two one-dollar coins for each team of three participants.
Here's how . . .	1. Divide the group into teams of three. 2. Give each team two one-dollar coins. 3. They have 5 minutes to decide between the three of them who will keep the coins. 4. If all else fails, a simple majority vote can decide. 5. After 5 minutes, any team still undecided will lose the coins back to you.
For example . . .	"We agreed Olivia would get both dollars. We trust she will donate them to her son's soccer team fund."

"We agreed Roger would get one, and Therese would get the other. They will let me be first to close my register the rest of the week."

"We agreed that Kenji would get both dollars. He gave each of us one-minute shoulder massages!"

Ask these questions . . .
> What strategies did you use during the negotiation? Which were most helpful?
> Did everyone rely on majority rules? Why or why not?
> How did the time limit influence how you negotiated? *(I felt rushed; It put more pressure on us; It made me cave in quicker; I was more aggressive; etc.)*
> How did you find out what the others valued? *(I just asked them what they wanted; I listened to what they were offering me and assumed they valued that; etc.)*
> What implications does this have for us back on the job?

Tips for success . . .
> Emphasize that this is not just an exercise. Whoever ends up with the coins gets to keep them.
> Two participants can end up with one coin each, or one participant can get both coins.
> Give a 2-minute warning before the play is to end.
> Most teams will not come up with the obviously easy solution: two participants collude and vote to award one coin to each of themselves. Explore why this did or did not happen during the Debrief and compare it to how things happen on the job.
> If one or two participants are not in a threesome, they can be Observers. The Observer role is to quietly watch the others participate. During the Debrief, the Observer shares his or her unique

observations. OR, have them create foursomes. The dynamics change considerably when there is an even number of participants using majority rules.

Try these variations . . .

- ➤ Give each team only one coin to negotiate.
- ➤ Use something other than money that all participants would value.
- ➤ Divide the group into pairs. Give each pair one coin to negotiate between them.

CARD TRIANGLES

This is . . .   A negotiation activity in which teams trade pieces of playing cards in hopes of finding complete cards.

The purpose is . . .   Participants learn to see others' perspectives before they can influence and persuade.

Use this when . . .
➤ Individuals are focusing too much on their own needs.
➤ Individuals need to hone their sales skills.
➤ Individuals need to develop their negotiation skills.

Materials you'll need . . .
➤ A deck of playing cards.
➤ Cut each card in half diagonally, then in half diagonally again, so each card is now in four triangle quarters.
➤ Mix all the pieces well, and place an equal number of pieces in the same number of envelopes as you will have teams.
➤ Small prizes for the winners (optional).

Here's how . . .
1. Divide the group into teams of three or four.
2. Give each team an envelope containing playing card triangles.
3. The teams have 3 minutes to examine and sort their pieces and plan their strategy for bartering.
4. Open the bartering. Everyone participates by bartering for the pieces their team needs. (They may barter individually or as a team.)

5. Allow 8 minutes for bartering.

6. Count the teams' completed cards, and announce the winning team.

Ask these questions . . .
- ➤ How willing were others to trade with you?
- ➤ What negotiation tactics were most successful for you? *(Seeing what they wanted and offering that; Being aggressive; Being a nice guy, etc.)*
- ➤ How did your strategy change during play? Why?
- ➤ What other skills did you have to draw on to be successful? *(Listening, empathy, giving a personal touch, creative problem solving, etc.)*
- ➤ In what work situations do we find ourselves negotiating for time, information, or resources?
- ➤ What implication does this have for us back on the job?

Tips for success . . .
- ➤ You must have at least three teams for this activity to work well. If necessary, have the teams consist of two participants.
- ➤ They can barter individually or as teams.
- ➤ Give a 2-minute warning before play is to end.
- ➤ Observe whether two or more teams combine might. Comment during the Debrief.

Try these variations . . .
- ➤ For smaller groups, give each participant an envelope, and have them all barter individually rather than in teams.
- ➤ After 4 minutes of play, give the teams 2 minutes to form a coalition. Any two teams that want to merge may do so before resuming play. Make sure there was an even number of teams to begin with. What influenced your team's decision to merge? And with whom?

LISTEN UP

This is . . .	A speaking activity in which participants listen as others share their views on a controversial topic.
The purpose is . . .	Participants practice listening skills, even when they are anxious to agree emphatically or strongly challenge.
Use this when . . .	➤ Individuals are not listening well. ➤ Individuals feel like others are not listening with open minds. ➤ Individuals want to get to know each other better.
Materials you'll need . . .	➤ An identical set of 10 to 15 index cards for each team. On each card in the set, you will have written a different controversial topic.
Here's how . . .	1. Have the participants pair up. 2. Give each pair a set of prepared index cards. 3. One partner draws a card and speaks for 3 minutes nonstop about her views on the topic. 4. Her partner may not say anything, just listen. 5. After 3 minutes, her partner has 1 minute to recap what he heard. This is not the time to rebut, debate, or agree—just summarize. 6. Reverse roles, and repeat with a new topic.
For example . . .	Controversial topics can include gay marriage, abortion, prayer in schools, euthanasia, election finance reform, capital punishment, income tax reform, needle exchange for drug users, unions, social security

reform, non-English-speaking communities in the USA, the space program, AIDS, nuclear arms, and so forth.

Ask these questions . . .

➤ How did the speakers' tone and body language contribute to the message?
➤ How did you feel listening without being able to speak your mind? *(Frustrated, anxious, made me listen better, etc.)*
➤ How did you feel speaking without your listener saying anything? *(Like I was being heard; Frustrated that I did not know where she was on the issue; etc.)*
➤ How was the listener's summary?
➤ When is it especially important for us to listen this attentively at work?
➤ What implication does this have for us back on the job?

Tips for success . . .

➤ Participants can reject up to two topics if they are uncomfortable discussing them.
➤ You can use one large set of index cards for the whole group. Duplicate cards are fine. Have enough cards for each participant (and a few extras). Distribute one card to each team. After one person has talked, distribute another card to the other participant. Do not give both cards at once. The second participant will be tempted to focus on what he may say when he should be listening to his partner!
➤ Give a 30-second warning before play is to end.

Try these variations . . .

➤ Choose the controversial topics so that they are all related to your industry, field, or organization.
➤ After the first participant speaks on a topic for 3 minutes, allow the second participant to speak

on the same topic for 3 minutes. Discuss how two monologues are different from one discussion.

➤ Allow the listener to speak, but only to ask questions to understand better the other's position.

ME, MYSELF, AND I

This is . . .	A story-telling activity that forces participants to communicate about anything except themselves.
The purpose is . . .	Participants see how often their communication is centered on themselves.
Use this when . . .	➤ Individuals need to improve their communication skills to focus less on self and more on others.
	➤ Individuals need to focus on listening skills.
	➤ Individuals need to practice creativity (around communication techniques).
	➤ You don't have prep time and/or materials for anything more elaborate.
Materials you'll need . . .	➤ No materials are necessary for this activity.
Here's how . . .	1. Have the participants pair up.
	2. One partner begins by speaking for 3 minutes nonstop. He must continue talking, no pauses.
	3. He may speak about any topic or several topics.
	4. He may never use the word "I."
	5. The listening partner may not speak at all, not even to ask questions or say "uh-huh."
	6. After his 3 minutes, reverse roles, and repeat.
Ask these questions . . .	➤ Which role was easier for you, the speaker or the listener? Why?

➤ How did you feel listening without being able to ask questions or contribute your own thoughts? *(Left out, less connected, more focused on the speaker, etc.)*

➤ How did you feel speaking without being able to check in with your listener? *(Worried that he was not understanding or did not care, uncomfortable with the attention on me, enjoying the attention and focus, etc.)*

➤ How difficult or easy was it to keep talking non-stop? Why?

➤ What creative ways did you find to talk about yourself without using "I?"

➤ How can we phrase our communications to focus better on the other person?

➤ What implications does this have for us back on the job?

Tips for success . . .

➤ Be prepared to demonstrate a portion of a 2-minute monologue without using "I" if the group demands it. Have the group try to catch you using an "I."

➤ Give a 30-second warning before the play ends.

Try these variations . . .

➤ Add a get-to-know-you element by having them determine who is the first speaker and listener by who is oldest, who lives furthest from your location, who has the next birthday, the cutest pet, is most physically fit, and so forth.

➤ Extend the speaking time to 5 minutes to make it more difficult.

➤ Add competitiveness by allowing the listeners to gain two points for each time the speaker says "I" and one point when they pause more than 5 seconds. Be prepared with small prizes for the winner(s). During the Debrief, ask how the competitiveness impacted the activity.

ORIGAMI

This is . . . An activity in which participants follow instructions to fold a sheet of paper while keeping their eyes closed.

The purpose is . . . Participants see how instructions can be interpreted differently, and thus how clear our communications need to be.

Use this when . . .
➤ Individuals are not communicating clearly or specifically.
➤ Individuals make too many assumptions of their listeners.
➤ You don't have prep time and/or materials for anything more elaborate.

Materials you'll need . . .
➤ One sheet of paper for each participant.

Here's how . . .
1. Give each participant a sheet of paper.
2. Announce that you will give them instructions on how to fold their paper.
3. Have them close their eyes. They must keep their eyes closed, and they may not ask questions during your instructions.
4. Give instructions to fold and rip their papers several times.
5. Have everyone open their eyes, unfold their papers, and compare what they look like.

For example . . .	➤ Fold your paper in half. ➤ Now, fold it in half again. ➤ Then, fold it in half one more time. ➤ Now, rip off the right corner. ➤ Turn your paper over and rip off the upper corner.
Ask these questions . . .	➤ Did everyone come up with the same end result? Why or why not? ➤ How would the results have been different if your eyes were left open? *(We could have compared and copied what others were doing; etc.)* ➤ How did you feel as I was giving the instructions? *(Confused, I wanted to ask questions, frustrated with you, etc.)* ➤ How could my instructions have been improved? ➤ What implication does this have for us back on the job?
Tips for success . . .	➤ Give the instructions slowly and deliberately. You are not trying to lose them or trick them. Repeat as necessary. ➤ Do not correct anyone as he or she is folding. There is no one right answer. The instructions are ambiguous on purpose. ➤ Watch to see if anyone opens his or her eyes. When is it appropriate to break the rules?
Try these variations . . .	➤ Invite participants to give the directions to the group. See if they can accomplish more consistent results after your Debrief. ➤ Allow the participants to keep their eyes open, but make the folding more complex. Use origami paper, and give the instructions for folding it into an origami shape.

SHARED VALUES

This is . . .	A sharing activity in which participants come to agreement on the most important shared values to the group.
The purpose is . . .	Participants come to agreement on the most important values they share.
Use this when . . .	➤ A significant project or work effort is beginning. ➤ Individuals feel like others are not listening with open minds. ➤ Individuals need to bond together.
Materials you'll need . . .	➤ Paper and a pen for each participant. ➤ One piece of flipchart paper for each team. ➤ Colored markers.
Here's how . . .	1. Have each participant take 2 minutes to write down what he or she feels are the three most important values to your organization. 2. Divide the group into teams of four to six participants. 3. Have each participant share her three values within her team. 4. From all the values shared, the team must agree on the top three most important values for your organization. 5. Give each team a piece of flipchart paper and some colored markers.

6. Each team creates a poster with words, symbols, and/or pictures that reflects those three values.
7. After 10 minutes, have each team present their poster to the group.

For example . . .
Values include things such as commitment to customers, integrity, teamwork, leadership, quality focus, innovation, efficiency, respect, creativity, learning, and so forth.

Ask these questions . . .
➤ What values seem to be common across teams?
➤ How did you handle disagreements in the teams?
➤ If someone new to the organization saw these lists of values, how do you think they would expect people to behave?
➤ Do we behave like that?
➤ What can cause us to lose sight of our values? *(Pressing deadlines, others acting differently, changes at work, etc.)* What can we do when that happens?
➤ How would living these values help us meet our goals?
➤ What implication does this have for us back on the job?

Tips for success . . .
➤ Encourage the teams to be creative in their representation of the values.
➤ If your organization already has stated values, have the teams still try to identify the three most important for this part of the organization.
➤ If a team does not finish, ask what prevented them from doing so. Others will learn from their difficulties. Then ask how those barriers could have been avoided or dealt with effectively.
➤ In the coming days, periodically ask which values are being demonstrated on the job.

Try these
variations . . .

➤ If your organization (or just your department) does not have a mission statement, have the teams make a poster to present what your mission statement should be. Remember, a mission statement explains why the organization exists, not its goals.

➤ If your organization (or just your department) does not have a vision statement, have the teams make a poster to present what your vision should be. Remember, the vision statement tells where you hope to be in the future.

WASHING MACHINES

This is . . .	A creative selling activity in which participants think of different ways to market a load of 10,000 used washing machines.
The purpose is . . .	Participants practice thinking of creative solutions and looking at things from others' perspectives.
Use this when . . .	➤ Individuals are focusing too much on their own needs. ➤ Creative thinking is not happening very much. ➤ Individuals need to hone their sales skills. ➤ You don't have prep time and/or materials for anything more elaborate.
Materials you'll need . . .	➤ No materials are necessary for this activity unless you give a small prize for the winning team.
Here's how . . .	1. Divide the group into teams of three to six participants. 2. Announce that each team has come upon a free load of 10,000 used old washing machines. 3. They are to think of a way to market these machines and prepare a sales pitch (a 30-second commercial) for the rest of the group. 4. Allow them 8 minutes to work in teams. 5. Each team presents its commercial to the rest of the group.

6. Have the group vote on which marketing design would most likely succeed in bringing in sales.

For example . . .
Some uses for the old machines may be as retro decorative planters; filled with ice and beer for parties; as a container for mixing dye for fabric; as huge, whimsical jack-in-the-boxes; as basketball hoops with a twist; as fishbowls for dark-loving fish; as a toy box; and so forth.

Ask these questions . . .
➤ How did your team arrive at the marketing design you chose?

➤ How creative do you think you were? Why?

➤ What assumptions did you operate under? *(That it had to do with laundry, that we must sell to consumers and not other businesses, that we could paint or otherwise alter the machines from their original state, etc.)* How did those assumptions limit or expand your creativity?

➤ How did you identify features and benefits of your product? (Point out that this is where you have to focus on others' needs.)

➤ What implication does this have for us back on the job?

Tips for success . . .
➤ Let each team determine if the washing machines are still operable or not.

➤ For a highly competitive group, rule that participants may not vote for their own design.

➤ Have one or two offbeat ideas yourself before the activity begins. If a team is really stuck, offer those ideas to help get their creative juices flowing.

➤ Emphasize that the commercial can be only 30 seconds long, and that you'll time it.

Try these variations . . .
➤ Rather than a 30-second commercial, each team creates a full-page magazine ad for their product

on a piece of flipchart paper. Explain to the group which magazine this would appear in and why.

➤ Rather than a 30-second commercial, each team creates a website for their product on a piece of flipchart paper. Explain to the group how the website works, and so forth.

➤ Rather than old used washing machines, try other unlikely items, such as old nonfunctioning computer monitors; beat up, old orange barrels from highway construction sites; the 1983 yellow pages for Key West, FL; and so forth.

CHAPTER 4

Connecting: Getting to Know Each Other

A DAY IN THE LIFE. . .

This is . . . An activity in which participants share with each other what their typical day looks like.

The purpose is . . . Participants learn new and interesting things about each other and connect with each other on a personal level.

Use this when . . .
➤ Individuals do not know each other very well.
➤ Individuals do not appreciate the each other's contributions.
➤ You don't have prep time and/or materials for anything more elaborate.

Materials you'll need . . .
➤ No materials are necessary for this activity.

Here's how . . .
1. Have the participants pair up.
2. One partner recalls in detail what his typical workday is like.
3. When listening, his partner can say only, "Then what?" or "Ooh, tell me more about that!"
4. After 5 minutes, reverse roles and repeat for 5 more minutes.

Ask these questions . . .
➤ How did you feel sharing these experiences with each other? (*I felt a sense of closeness; I realized we have more in common; Empathy; etc*)

> What did you learn about your partner and his workload?

> What implication does this have for us back on the job?

Tips for success . . .

> Five minutes may seem long to some. They will be tempted to finish in a minute or two. That is not enough time to share the detail the listener needs to get a good sense of what his partner's day is really like. Remember, the objective is not to give an overview and be finished; the objective is to understand each other's workload better.

> If they struggle with describing a typical day (because it is never "typical"), have them describe yesterday.

> If you will not be participating, begin the activity by demonstrating how to do it. Share with the group your typical day!

> Give a 1-minute time check before the 5 minutes are up.

Try these variations . . .

> To get to know each other on a personal basis, have the participants focus on a weekend or other nonwork day.

> After the participants share their days, have them pair up with someone else and repeat the activity.

> Have the participants share their days in teams of three to six. This takes longer, but allows them to hear and learn from more than just one or two other participants.

GOSSIP TIME

This is . . . An activity in which participants share fun or complimentary gossip about each other and then try to guess who said what.

The purpose is . . . Participants learn new and interesting things about each other. This may prompt further appreciation for each other and stronger personal ties.

Use this when . . .
- ➤ Individuals know each other quite well.
- ➤ There is a comfortable trust among the group.
- ➤ You don't have prep time and/or materials for anything more elaborate.

Materials you'll need . . .
- ➤ Paper and pencils or pens for each participant.

Here's how . . .
1. One person volunteers (or is volunteered!) to be the first Target.
2. Everyone else writes one thing about the Target on a slip of paper. It can be complimentary or a bit surprising.
3. Collect the statements, and randomly select one to read aloud.
4. The Target gets one chance to guess who wrote it.
5. If the Target guesses incorrectly, read the next statement. Each time a statement is read, the Target has one chance to guess its author.
6. Play continues until the Target can correctly identify the source of a particular statement.

7. When the Target correctly identifies the author, that author becomes the next Target, and another round begins from step 2.
8. Play as many rounds as time allows or until energy for the activity wanes.

For example . . .
"Someone says you are still in love with Ringo Starr!"
"Someone called you a good listener."
"Someone says you sing great karaoke."

Ask these questions . . .
➤ How much did you learn about each other?
➤ How embarrassed (or proud) were you when you were the Target?
➤ What made it difficult (or easy) for you to guess who authored the comments?

Tips for success . . .
➤ Keep the mood light and fun. Protect the group from mean or inappropriate remarks.
➤ Don't let the Target read the papers. He or she may be able to identify the source by the handwriting.
➤ You may ask the Target to leave the room while the others write.
➤ If time is limited, you don't have to wait for every person to write something. Ask the Target to leave the room during writing, so he or she cannot see who doesn't turn in a paper.

Try these variations . . .
➤ Limit the comments to only work-related or even project-related items.
➤ If you limit the comments to only complimentary items, this becomes a Recognition activity.
➤ You can focus this activity on a particular learning goal. Limit the comments to the Target's communication style, interpersonal relationships, teamwork, and problem-solving abilities or techniques or other work-related goals.

HUMAN BILLBOARDS

This is . . .   A self-disclosure activity in which participants create a poster about themselves.

The purpose is . . .   Participants learn more about each other and connect on a personal level.

Use this when . . .
- ➤ Individuals do not know each other very well.
- ➤ One or more of the individuals are new to the team.
- ➤ A new team is forming.

Materials you'll need . . .
- ➤ One flipchart paper for each participant.
- ➤ Colored markers.
- ➤ Scissors.

Here's how . . .
1. Give each participant a piece of flipchart paper and some colored markers.
2. They have 6 minutes to use words, pictures, or symbols to describe themselves on the "billboard."
3. Cut a slit or an "X" near the top of the paper so the participant can fit his or her head through it.
4. Participants put their billboard on so it drapes in front of them.
5. Encourage them to mingle for 6 minutes.
6. While mingling, they can only ask questions about another's billboard or respond to questions asked of them.

Ask these	➤ Why is it important for us to know each other
questions . . .	outside of a purely work-related context?
	➤ How difficult (or easy) was it to share information
	about yourself with others?
	➤ How can we learn more about each other back on
	the job?

Tips for	➤ Reassure those who are reluctant and those who
success . . .	do not know what to write that they only need to
	share what they are comfortable disclosing now.
	➤ Have them print their names on their billboards
	and post them around the break room, conference
	room, or lunchroom so they can refer to them and
	continue to reach out to others.
	➤ You may use this activity to just get acquainted or
	get a meeting started without asking the Debrief
	questions afterwards.
	➤ You can use this activity more than once with the
	same group. Use one of the Variations below.

Try these	➤ Direct what will go on the billboard. It can be
variations . . .	centered on one theme, for example, only career
	related; only company/organization related; only
	non-work-related; only favorites—color, food,
	book, movie, US President, and so forth; only
	wishes and dreams, and so forth.
	➤ Instead of a billboard, have participants create a
	screen saver, T-shirt, bumper sticker, personal flag,
	license plate, tattoo, and so forth.
	➤ You may use regular 8½ × 11 paper instead of
	flipchart paper and have participants tape them
	to their chests.
	➤ You may use tape and string to make a neck
	holder for the billboard, rather than cutting it.

MY N.A.M.E.

This is . . .   An activity in which participants introduce themselves by presenting their first names as acronyms.

The purpose is . . .   Everyone knows everyone else's name and some interesting things about each other. That information may prompt some small talk later.

Use this when . . .
- One or more of the individuals' names are not known.
- Individuals do not know each other very well.
- You don't have prep time and/or materials for anything more elaborate.

Materials you'll need . . .
- No materials are necessary for this activity.

Here's how . . .
1. Give the group 5 minutes to think of interesting facts about themselves that correspond to the letters of their first name.
2. Have each participant share his or her acronym.

For example . . .   "Hi, I'm Logan. L is for Led Zepplin, one of my favorite rock groups. O is for Ohio, which is where I live. G is for German, the only foreign language I know. A is for Aunt Wendee, my favorite relative. And N is for Nice, because I am a nice guy!"

Ask these questions . . .
- Why is it important for us to know each other beyond a purely work-related context?

➤ How difficult (or easy) was it to share information about yourself with others?

➤ How can we learn more about each other back on the job?

Tips for success . . .

➤ If participants get stuck, tell them they do not have to follow the rules strictly. For example, "L" can be for Loving chocolate, Loving chess, Loving snow, and so forth.

➤ Be prepared to share your own acronym as an example for the group.

➤ You may use this activity to just get acquainted or get a meeting started without asking the Debrief questions afterwards.

Try these variations . . .

➤ Instead of acronyms about themselves, have the participants make acronyms from their first names that correspond to the kind of work they do (customer service, research, etc.) or a current project they are working on or a problem they collectively face (you may be surprised at a few creative ideas for resolution!).

A PENNY FOR YOUR THOUGHTS

This is . . .	A light introduction activity that reveals a quick, personal fact about each participant.
The purpose is . . .	Everyone knows everyone else's name and one interesting fact about each other. That information may prompt some small talk later.
Use this when . . .	➤ One or more of the individual's names are not known. ➤ Individuals do not know each other very well. ➤ You don't have prep time and/or materials for anything more elaborate.
Materials you'll need . . .	➤ One penny for each participant. The best pennies are shiny, easy to read, and less than 20 years old.
Here's how . . .	1. Give a penny to each participant. (As you're doing this, jokingly ask if they realized that they were going to receive a "cash bonus" for attending today!). 2. Ask them first to introduce themselves with their name and any other information you want shared with the group. 3. Then ask them to share something significant or interesting about themselves from the year on their penny. 4. You go first to set the example.

For **example . . .**	"Hi, I'm Ruth. I've been at this company 14 years and in this department for 3 years. My penny says 1999, and that's the year I let my husband talk me into going skydiving with him!"
Ask these **questions . . .**	➤ Why is it important for us to know more about each other? ➤ How difficult (or easy) was it to share information about yourself with others? ➤ How can we learn more about each other back on the job?
Tips for **success . . .**	➤ Give them a moment to think of something to say before beginning. ➤ When you want them to share more than two pieces of information besides their name, list what you want on a chart or board. ➤ If someone says she can't remember anything significant from that year, encourage her to describe what was going on in her life at that time (where she was living, what job she had, hobbies she was pursuing, etc.) OR, use one of the variations below. ➤ This activity can be used with the same group more than once (since participants are unlikely to get the same year a second time). ➤ If you don't have pennies, participants can just pull coins out of their own pockets or purses. ➤ You may use this activity to just get acquainted or get a meeting started without asking the Debrief questions afterwards.
Try these **variations . . .**	➤ Have participants explain what would be different if they could relive that year OR how their lives would be different if that year never happened. ➤ Have participants tell what their favorite song, movie, TV show, or other entertainment was from that year.

- ➤ Don't use pennies; just have the participants tell what the best year of their life was and why.
- ➤ If you have time, let the group ask questions after each participant shares her information (*Had your husband been skydiving before? Where did you dive? Have you done it since? Would you even want to?* And so on).

? RATHER THAN

This is . . .	A light introductory activity that reveals personal preferences about each participant.
The purpose is . . .	Everyone knows one personal preference about each other. That information may then prompt some small talk later.
Use this when . . .	➤ One or more of the individuals are new to the team. ➤ Individuals do not know each other very well. ➤ You don't have prep time and/or materials for anything more elaborate.
Materials you'll need . . .	➤ No materials are necessary for this activity.
Here's how . . .	1. Sit in a circle so everyone can see each other if possible. 2. Start by declaring something that you like to do. 3. The participant next to you restates what you said and then says something that he would *rather* do than that. 4. The next participant restates what was just said and then says something that *she* would rather do than that. 5. Continue around the room.
For example . . .	"I like to collect porcelain dolls." "Rather than collect porcelain dolls, I like to eat ice cream."

"Rather than eat ice cream, I like to sunbathe on the beach."
"Rather than sunbathe on the beach, I like to surf the Net."
"Rather than surf the Net, I like to coach my daughter's soccer team."

Ask these questions . . .

- ➤ Why is it important for us to know each other beyond a purely work-related context?
- ➤ How difficult (or easy) was it to share information about yourself with others?
- ➤ How can we learn more about each other back on the job?

Tips for success . . .

- ➤ Play can go around the room indefinitely.
- ➤ Allow the group to react briefly to comments but not to dwell on anyone's statement (and certainly not to criticize)—however bizarre or unpopular!
- ➤ You may use this activity to just get acquainted or get a meeting started without asking the Debrief questions afterwards.

Try these variations . . .

- ➤ Specify a category (such as related only to your team and its work, related only to your company/organization, only non-work-related, only related to hobbies, etc.).
- ➤ Make this an ice breaker/introductory activity by merely asking the participants to preface their Rather Than comment with their name. For example, "My name is Derek, and rather than eat ice cream. . ."
- ➤ Play Worse Than. Declare something you don't like. The next participant declares that worse than that, would be something that would be worse for him. For example, "Worse than going to the dentist would be getting lost in a new city."

READY, SET, REORGANIZE!

This is . . . An activity in which participants organize themselves based on various pieces of information about themselves.

The purpose is . . . Participants learn new and interesting facts about each other. That information may then prompt some small talk later.

Use this when . . .
- One or more of the individuals are new to the team.
- Individuals do not know each other very well.
- You don't have prep time and/or materials for anything more elaborate.

Materials you'll need . . .
- No materials are necessary for this activity.

Here's how . . .
1. Divide the group in half. Stand in lines facing each other.
2. Announce a category (for example, first name).
3. Both teams reorganize themselves alphabetically by first name as quickly as possible.
4. Announce another category (for example, home street address name).
5. Both teams reorganize themselves in this new alphabetical order as quickly as possible.
6. Repeat for as many categories as you want.

For example . . .	Additional sorting categories could be last name, birthday (chronologically), favorite food, pet's name, length of time at current organization (numerically), birthplace (alphabetically or geographically from east to west), fantasy vacation destination, formal job title, number of USA states visited in lifetime (numerically), and so forth.
Ask these questions . . .	➤ Why is it important for us to know each other beyond a purely work-related context? ➤ How difficult (or easy) was it to share information about yourself with others? ➤ What surprises did you have when reorganizing yourselves? ➤ How can we learn more about each other back on the job?
Tips for success . . .	➤ Think of more categories than you think you will need. It is better to have too many than not enough. ➤ Stop the game when the energy or enthusiasm starts to fade. ➤ This game can be played again with different categories or when a new member joins the team. ➤ You may use this activity to just get acquainted or get a meeting started without asking the Debrief questions afterwards.
Try these variations . . .	➤ If the group is large (more than 24 participants), divide into three competing teams. ➤ Give small prizes for the team that is fastest. ➤ Halfway through the game, the teams combine into one line for a category. Once they have sorted themselves, divide them in half at the midpoint of the long line. They now are two new

teams. Continue the game, and they get to know new participants on their team.

➤ Keep the group in one group for all sorting.

➤ If the enthusiasm is high, ask the group to come up with a category to try.

SIMILARITIES AND DIFFERENCES

This is . . .   An introductory activity in which participants are challenged to find how they are similar and different from each other.

The purpose is . . .   Participants learn new and interesting things about each other and connect with each other on a personal level.

Use this when . . .
- Individuals do not know each other very well.
- A significant project or work effort is beginning.
- Individuals do not appreciate each other very much.

Materials you'll need . . .
- An index card (or sheet of paper) and a pen for each participant.

Here's how . . .
1. Give each participant an index card and a pen.
2. Have them divide their cards into three columns headed by "Name, Similar, and Different."
3. Have them mingle and try to fill their card with as many names as possible.
4. For each name, they find something that they have in common with the other person and one way they are different.

For example . . .	Name	Similar	Different
	1. Tim	We love to travel.	He likes country music.
	2. Benjamin	We like to snuggle with loved ones.	He speaks Spanish.
	3. Maria	We watch "The Simpsons."	She plays an instrument.
	4. Gail	We love to read.	She doesn't travel much.
	5. Wayne	We lift weights regularly.	He doesn't have any pets.
	6. Heidee	We love to cook.	I don't collect anything.

Ask these questions . . .

➤ How difficult (or easy) was it to share information about yourself with others?

➤ What surprises did you have finding similarities and differences?

➤ How can we learn more about each other back on the job?

Tips for success . . .

➤ Encourage the participants to not duplicate any answers. If you find a second person with whom you share a love of chocolate, try to find something else you also have in common with that person.

➤ Encourage them to have their Similarities and Differences be unrelated. For example, if the Similarity is "we both love music," rather than "he likes rap and I don't" as the Difference, try for something unrelated to music altogether.

➤ You may use this activity to just get acquainted or get a meeting started without asking the Debrief questions afterwards.

Try these
variations . . .

➤ Limit similarities and differences to only work-related items or only personal items.

➤ Divide the group into teams of four to six participants. Have each team find one thing all members have in common and where all members differ. After a few minutes, shuffle the teams, and repeat.

SWEET STORIES

This is . . . An activity in which participants share a story about themselves based on the color of the candy they have in their hands.

The purpose is . . . Participants learn more about each other and learn to trust each other a little more.

Use this when . . .
- ➤ One or more individuals are new to the group.
- ➤ Individuals do not know each other very well.
- ➤ The group knows each other very well (see variation below).

Materials you'll need . . .
- ➤ A large bag of M&Ms®, Skittles®, or other colored candy pieces.

Here's how . . .
1. Have each participant take one candy.
2. Do not eat it yet!
3. Take turns sharing with the group a story based on the following code:
   - ➤ Blue candy: A time at work when you felt very proud.
   - ➤ Green candy: A boss you respected and why.
   - ➤ Yellow candy: A reason you are proud to belong to this organization.
   - ➤ Brown candy: An embarrassing moment at work.
   - ➤ Orange candy: A time at work when you failed.

> ➤ Purple candy: A funny thing that happened to you at work.
> ➤ Red candy: A time at work when you were scared.

4. Eat the candy.

Ask these questions . . .
> ➤ Why is it important for us to learn about each other at work?
> ➤ How difficult (or easy) was it to share information about yourself with others?
> ➤ How can we learn more about each other back on the job?

Tips for success . . .
> ➤ Other categories can be used that relate more closely to the workload, organization, or special project.
> ➤ The stories do not have to be "the most" any-thing—the most embarrassing, the most funny, and so forth. Take that pressure away. Allow participants to share the kind of story they are comfortable sharing with the group.
> ➤ If you use a candy other than M&Ms®, be sure to adjust the color coding to match the colors of what you use.
> ➤ This activity can be repeated. Just ask for different stories! Or start every meeting with one person telling a story, and over time you will hear from everyone.
> ➤ Limit the length of stories so no one monopolizes the time.
> ➤ Post the story color code so participants can easily match their candy to the story they need to tell.

Try these variations . . .
> ➤ Divide larger groups (more than 12 participants) into smaller teams to share their stories with each other.

- ➤ Remove the words "at work" for each color, and get to know each other better personally.
- ➤ Divide the group into small groups of three to five participants. Give them several minutes to share their stories from one color. Select the best story from the team, and share with the larger group.
- ➤ Use only two categories. Toss a coin to determine which story to tell.
- ➤ For the group that knows each other very well, have them tell the stories about each other rather than about themselves.
- ➤ Get to know each other on a personal level along lines such as these: one thing you learned from your parents, why you like your favorite movie, tell about your kitchen at home, pets you have (or have had), and so forth.

CHAPTER 5

Cooperation: Working Together as a Team

CATCH!

This is . . .	A fast-paced ball-tossing game where participants are encouraged to improve the time it takes to pass the ball around the group.
The purpose is . . .	The group sees that improvements can always be made on a process, and that it takes the whole team to make process improvement work.
Use this when . . .	➤ The group needs to be looking to itself (rather than the boss) for ways to improve.
	➤ A feeling of arrogance (*"We can't get much better than this!"*) is strong in the group.
	➤ Group members are not cooperating with each other as well as they should.
Materials you'll need . . .	➤ A Koosh® ball, beanbag, or similar item that is safe to toss.
	➤ A stopwatch, watch, or clock with a second hand.
Here's how . . .	1. Arrange the group in a large circle with everyone standing.
	2. Give the ball to anyone.
	3. Ask him to throw the ball to anyone in the circle.
	4. The catcher now throws the ball to someone else in the circle.
	5. This continues as each participant always throws the ball to someone who has not had it yet.
	6. The last one throws the ball back to the partici-

pant who had it first. The group has established their Pattern.

7. Have them repeat the same Pattern throwing the ball to the same person, in the same order as they did before. Time them.
8. If anyone drops the ball, it goes back to the first participant to start again. Time keeps ticking.
9. Announce the time, and ask them how much faster they think they can get.
10. Repeat the Pattern, and time them again.
11. Give them 3 minutes to create a strategy to vastly improve their time again.
12. Repeat the Pattern and time them again.

For example . . . There is no appropriate example for this activity.

Ask these questions . . .
➤ How did you feel the first time I timed you? On subsequent timings? *(Nervous, energized, competitive, pressured, etc.)*
➤ What strategies did you employ to improve your speed? How successful were they?
➤ What assumptions or limits did you impose on yourselves? *(We had to stay in the same circle order we were in. We had to catch with our hands [not laps, if sitting]; etc.)*
➤ How did you feel when participant X dropped the ball? *(Frustrated, angry, depressed, hopeless, empathetic, etc.)*
➤ What was the key to your success?
➤ What implication does this have for us back on our jobs?

Tips for success . . .
➤ Help them be successful. If they forget who gets the ball next, remind them. Just be careful not to take over leadership for the group.

- Be supportive of whoever drops the ball if the group is not.
- Do not offer suggestions on how to improve; let them struggle with it. One of the best ways is for them to rearrange their positions in the circle!
- Watch, and listen to their comments during the activity. Bring up relevant ones during the Debrief.
- Post the rules of the game so participants can refer to them while they play.

Try these variations . . .

- Establish two different patterns in the group with two different colored balls. Time them accomplishing both patterns at the same time.
- Form two groups (each with one ball), and do them simultaneously. See if the groups compete more against their own time (which is the stated objective) or against each other's times. Ask how the competitive pressure helps or hinders their efforts on the job.
- Make this more about dealing with change by asking them to reverse the flow of the ball after a round or two, but still maintain the same or better speed.
- For smaller groups, have them also say their name, a color, a company product, and so forth as they toss the ball.

PASS THE CARD

This is . . .	A quick moving activity in which participants pass cards from one to another in a relay.
The purpose is . . .	Teamwork and the competitive spirit energize participants during times of change.
Use this when . . .	➤ The group needs an energizer before or during a draining or very long meeting. ➤ Individuals would benefit from a shot of competitiveness. ➤ Group members are not cooperating with each other as well as they should.
Materials you'll need . . .	➤ One deck of playing cards for each team. ➤ A prize for the fastest team (optional).
Here's how . . .	1. Divide the group into teams of four to eight participants. 2. Each team sits on chairs in a line side by side. 3. Place a deck of cards on the floor next to the chair at the far right end of each team's line. 4. Give the instructions, and allow teams 5 minutes to plan their strategy. 5. To play, the participant nearest the deck picks up a card. 6. He then passes the card from his left hand to the right hand of the participant to his left.

7. The second participant passes that card to her left hand, then on to the right hand of the next participant.

8. Play continues like this until the last participant places the card in a pile on the floor next to her with her left hand.

9. No one may hold more than one card at a time.

10. The first team with all cards stacked at the end of their line wins.

For example . . .

As soon as the first participant gets rid of that first card, he can reach down and get the next one to start passing. He does not have to wait for the first card to travel all the way down his line.

Ask these questions . . .

➤ How did you determine your strategy? Did it work?

➤ How did you feel when a participant dropped a card? *(Angry, worried about time, impatient, frustrated, empathetic, etc.)*

➤ Which strategies worked best?

➤ When do we have to be this much in sync at work?

➤ What implications does this have for our team back on the job?

Tips for success . . .

➤ Use this opportunity to mix the group up. Arrange teams so that participants who do not normally work together are on the same team.

➤ As much as possible, have the teams lined up so they can easily see each other. This will increase the competitive nature and also provide distractions!

➤ Post game rules so participants can refer to them during play.

Try these
variations . . .

➤ Make this more difficult by blindfolding some (just the first and last?) or all participants.

➤ Items other than the cards may be used: pennies, paperclips, items unique to your workplace, and so forth.

➤ Make this more difficult by using pads of sticky notes. Require that the pad be reconstructed at the end of the team line!

POPCORN

This is . . . A fun activity in which participants, working in pairs, feed each other pieces of popcorn on a spoon while both are blindfolded.

The purpose is . . . Participants learn to cooperate with each other, have fun, and reinforce communication skills.

Use this when . . .
- Individuals need to slow down and focus.
- Individuals are not being creative at problem solving.
- The group needs to loosen up, have some fun, and laugh.

Materials you'll need . . .
- A blindfold for each participant.
- A spoon for each participant.
- Popcorn.

Here's how . . .
1. Have the participants pair up.
2. Distribute blindfolds, spoons, and popcorn to everyone.
3. While both are blindfolded, one participant feeds 10 pieces of popcorn to his or her partner on the spoon one at a time.
4. After they are successful, reverse roles and repeat.

For example . . . There is no appropriate example for this activity.

Ask these questions . . .
- How did you feel when you put on the blindfold? *(Nervous, disoriented, etc.)* Why?

> What happened as you tried to feed each other? *(Popcorn kept blowing off the spoon; She jabbed my nose with the spoon; I had to feel my way; etc.)*

> What ways did you find to communicate, cooperate, and be successful? *(Touch, frequent feedback, overhearing what someone else did that worked, etc.)*

> What implications does this have for us back on the job?

Tips for success . . .

> Prepare by putting small amounts of popcorn in plastic bags for each participant. Some of the popcorn will be dropped, so put more than 10 pieces in each bag!

> Supply something other than popcorn if you know someone is allergic to it.

> Watch to see if anyone cheats with the blindfolds. When is it appropriate to break the rules?

Try these variations . . .

> Easier, and perhaps tastier, would be small candies.

> Have the participants alternate feeding each other one piece of popcorn instead of all 10 in a row.

> Divide the group into teams of three or more, and have each team member feed the popcorn to the person on the right simultaneously. This is much more difficult and requires much more cooperation and teamwork.

> Use forks to stab the popcorn, instead of spoons.

PUZZLED

This is . . .   An activity in which participants learn, as they assemble a puzzle, that other teams have some pieces they need, and they have pieces others need.

The purpose is . . .   Participants see that cooperation across real or perceived team boundaries can be beneficial (sometimes even crucial) for success.

Use this when . . .
- ➤ The group needs to cooperate within itself or with other groups to be successful.
- ➤ Competitiveness is hindering team efforts.
- ➤ Individuals are asking the boss to solve their problems for them.

Materials you'll need . . .
- ➤ One children's puzzle for each small group, preferably with 20–50 pieces.
- ➤ A bag (or box or envelope) for each puzzle's pieces.
- ➤ Assemble the puzzle bags in advance (without the group knowing you have done this):
  - a. Place all the puzzle pieces for each puzzle in a separate bag.
  - b. Line up the filled bags in front of you.
  - c. Remove two to three pieces from each bag.
  - d. Place those pieces in other bags, each piece in a different bag.

Here's how . . .   1. Divide the group into teams of three to six participants. There must be the same number of teams as you have bags of puzzles.

2. Give each team a bag of puzzle pieces.
3. Do not disclose that the bags have been tampered with.
4. Tell the participants that their objective is to put the puzzles together in less than 5 minutes.
5. Have them begin.

For example . . .

➤ If they ask for help, decline. Encourage them to use what resources are available to accomplish their objective. Tell them, "All the pieces necessary to accomplish your objective are out."

➤ If they ask permission to work with other groups, be noncommittal. Say, "You know what your objective is; do what you need to do to achieve it!"

Ask these questions . . .

➤ What assumptions did you make at the beginning of this activity? *(We had all the pieces for our puzzle in this bag; We were in a race; We did not need any outside help; etc.)*

➤ Why did you feel this was a competition? *(Conditioned, my natural style, etc.)*

➤ How did you react when you realized you did not have all the pieces you needed? *(Frustrated, angry, lost, etc.)* How did you deal with it then?

➤ How did you feel when other groups came offering pieces or asking for some of your pieces? *(Imposed upon, go away, rushed, confused, etc.)*

➤ How is this similar to our work? *(We ask you for help when we could solve something ourselves; We see everything as a competition; etc.)*

➤ What implications does this have for you back on your jobs?

Tips for success . . .

➤ Be sure that no two puzzles are exactly the same; otherwise, the value of swapping the pieces may be lost.

> When the first team discovers they are missing a piece, they may look to you for an explanation. Calmly remind them of their objective (to put the puzzles together), and announce that all the puzzle pieces *are* out.

> Do not make the types of encouraging comments that may lead them to believe they are in competition *(Oh, this team is going to win; You guys better hurry up; etc.).*

Try these
variations . . .

> Replace the puzzles with Lego® building sets (and their instruction sheets) having, preferably, fewer than 80 pieces.

> Make the puzzles yourself out of thick (or laminated) paper. This is especially good if you want the completed puzzles to say something—quotes or messages that will help you segue into the meeting's main topic or focus.

SILENCE IS GOLDEN

This is . . .   An activity in which small groups draw their vision of an ideal work environment without speaking to each other.

The purpose is . . .   Participants see how much of what they communicate is conveyed without words.

Use this when . . .
- Individuals are not communicating well with customers, suppliers, partners, and so forth.
- Minor conflict is arising in the group because of voice tone or nonverbal cues, not the actual words being used ("all I said was. . .").
- Language barriers or hearing impairments confront the group.

Materials you'll need . . .
- Colored markers for each group.
- A piece of flipchart paper for each group.
- Tape to post the drawings.

Here's how . . .
1. Divide the group into teams of four to six participants.
2. Give each group a piece of flipchart paper and some markers.
3. Have each team draw a floor plan or a picture of the ideal work environment for the group. Money is no object, so be creative and have fun with this one!
4. Participants may not talk to anyone while planning or drawing.

5. After 10 minutes, have each team share their drawing with the group.

Ask these questions . . .
➤ What did the drawings have in common?
➤ How did you communicate with each other? *(Acted things out, drew small pictures on scrap paper, Wrote notes, etc.)*
➤ How accurate were you in communicating with each other, even though you could not use words? (They will probably be surprised at how effectively they were able to communicate and work together without words.)
➤ What implications does this have for us back on the job?

Tips for success . . .
➤ Studies have shown that 7% of what is communicated is done with words, 38% with tone of voice, and 55% with nonverbal clues. For telephone conversations, 18% of the content is communicated through words and 82% through tone.
➤ Decide before the activity if you will allow the group to write notes (using words) to communicate.
➤ As they work, observe what they do that is effective, and bring them out during the Debrief.
➤ Give a 1-minute warning before time is up.

Try these variations . . .
➤ Use molding clay or building blocks instead of the paper and markers.
➤ To emphasize the importance of tone of voice (for those who spend much time on phones), allow the participants to talk only with their mouths closed. Their lips will never open, but they can grunt and make other noises with their voice box. The tone will come through!
➤ Have them draw a solution to a problem your organization currently faces. This will be more difficult and may require more time.

STAR POWER

This is . . .	An activity in which participants form a star shape with a long piece of rope.
The purpose is . . .	Participants learn to cooperate with each other, have fun, and reinforce communication skills.
Use this when . . .	➤ Individuals are not cooperating well. ➤ A new group is forming and needs to come together. ➤ The group needs to loosen up, have some fun, and laugh.
Materials you'll need . . .	➤ One 40- to 50-foot rope.
Here's how . . .	1. Have all participants pick up the rope. 2. They can move their hands along the rope, but they cannot change places with each other. 3. They must form a five-pointed star with the rope in 10 minutes with no rope left over at either end.
For example . . .	The star may be just the outline of a star or one in which the lines cross over each other, like a star drawn without a pen ever leaving the paper.
Ask these questions . . .	➤ How does this activity relate to teamwork? *(We had to cooperate; We had to agree on things; We had to support the final outcome; We had to listen to each other; etc.)*

➤ How did you deal with everyone's ideas about the way to proceed?

➤ Did anyone emerge as the leader? How did they function?

➤ How did you handle disagreements?

➤ What implications does this have for us back on the job?

Tips for success . . .

➤ You may want to post a drawing of the star for easy reference. Remember, this will help the team (and you may not want to do that!).

➤ For larger groups (more than 20 participants), form two groups, and have two ropes, OR, simply use a longer rope. Have at least 2–3 feet of length per participant.

Try these variations . . .

➤ Have them try another shape, a letter, a word, or your organization's logo.

➤ Blindfold the participants. If you blindfold them all, make the shape much simpler—a square or triangle will be difficult enough. How did the group learn to "see?"

➤ Require that the activity be accomplished without speaking. How did the group manage to communicate? Or, let some speak and some not. How did the group leverage those who could not speak?

➤ Select a leader, and blindfold only that person. How did the leader and group overcome the handicap?

TIED!

This is . . .   A simple activity in which the participants try to cross the finish line at exactly the same time.

The purpose is . . .   Participants see how an activity that looks simple, when it involves coordinating others, rarely is.

Use this when . . .
- Individuals are breezing through tasks, underestimating what needs to be done.
- Individuals need to slow down and focus.
- Individuals are not cooperating well.

Materials you'll need . . .
- A long rope or tape to represent a start line and a finish line (optional—a highly visible line in the carpet or flooring may work fine).

Here's how . . .
1. Line the group up behind a starting line.
2. On your signal, they are to proceed to the finish line.
3. They must all cross the finish line at exactly the same time.
4. If they are not all together, they need to go back to the starting line and try again.
5. They need to keep trying until they succeed.

For example . . .   Participants might use a military cadence, a countdown, holding hands, or some other clever coordination technique, but usually only after their first efforts fail.

Ask these **questions . . .**	➤ How easy did this sound at first? *(Simple, piece of cake, etc.)*
	➤ How easy was it? *(Harder to coordinate than we thought, etc.)*
	➤ When have we thought something at work was easy at first and then discovered it was harder to coordinate (especially when it involved the efforts of others)?
	➤ What implications does this have for us on the job?
Tips for **success . . .**	➤ Once the activity begins, no participant can stop motion (this eliminates the clever ruse of having everyone get up to the finish line and stop and wait to just take one step together!).
	➤ This is harder than it seems. Depending on the size of the group, it will generally take 5–10 attempts to succeed.
Try these **variations . . .**	➤ Make it more difficult by allowing the participants to look only straight ahead or at the ceiling.
	➤ Have them do the activity while walking backwards.

UNITED HEARTS

This is . . .   A fast-paced card game in which teams feel a need to compete for points when, actually, they could all win through cooperation.

The purpose is . . .   Participants see that competitiveness among them can be detrimental, and flexibility is critical for success.

Use this when . . .
> The group members need to cooperate with each other or with other groups to be successful.
> Competitiveness is hindering team efforts.
> Individuals need to understand the value of being flexible with plans and strategies.

Materials you'll need . . .
> One deck of playing cards for every 15 participants.

Here's how . . .
1. Divide the group into three teams of two to five participants. Equal sized teams are not critical.
2. Keep the hearts, and give each team an entire suit of cards. They may look at their cards during play.
3. Each team's objective is to earn 30 points. As the Dealer, you are not playing for points.
4. Each team must designate one member to be their Leader.
5. Explain the rules below, and give them 3 minutes to plan their strategy.

6. There will be 13 rounds (one for each card in everyone's hand). For each round, you will play any heart card face up on the table. Then each team Leader selects a card and places it face down on the table.

7. Once the Leaders have all played, flip the cards over. The card with the highest value (excluding your heart) wins the heart points for that team. For example, if the highest card played is the 8 of clubs, and the heart is a 10, the clubs team gets 10 points.

8. Numbered cards are worth face value; jacks are worth 11 points, queens 12, kings 13, and aces 1 point.

9. If the high card is a tie, the heart points are lost that round.

10. As cards are played, they are out of play for the remainder of the game.

11. Once play begins, no one may speak.

12. After five rounds, and again after the ninth round, allow the teams 2 minutes to regroup and discuss their progress.

13. Determine which teams earned 30 points.

For example . . . If the 4 of clubs, 5 of spades, and 9 of diamonds are played for the jack of hearts, the diamonds team gets 11 points.

If the 4 of clubs, 9 of spades, and 9 of diamonds are played for the jack of hearts, none of the teams will get the 11 points; they are lost forever.

If the 4 of clubs, 4 of spades, and 9 of diamonds are played for the jack of hearts, the diamonds team gets 11 points.

Ask these questions . . .
➤ What happened?
➤ How did you select your Leader?

- What strategy did you have? How did you select it?
- (If no one has said this yet,) how many points were possible altogether? *(91 points)* So, all three teams could have been successful with a win–win–win solution, right? (Expect surprised looks and smiles as they realize they competed when they did not have to.)
- Why did you compete with each other? *(We assumed it was a competition; We did not want to trust them; We are conditioned to compete; etc.)*
- What implications does this have for our team back on the job? (Do not let your sales force or similar group lose the lesson here. Even they need to realize that, internally, they are not in competition with others for resources or support, etc.)

Tips for success . . .

- If there are more than 15 participants, extra participants can act as Observers, or two (or more) separate games can be played simultaneously. Designate a Dealer at each table, who will follow your lead. Remind the Dealers that they are not playing for points.
- If the teams ask about collaborating together, allow it! Even if they figure this out, it will take cooperation and trust to make it happen.
- The rule states that they cannot talk. There is no rule against pointing, grunting, facial expressions, writing, or otherwise communicating with each other.
- Be careful not to suggest that the first team to get 30 points is better off than others.
- Be careful not to suggest that points beyond 30 are of any value.
- Post the rules so participants can refer to them during play.

Try these variations . . .

➤ Play a second round, and see if the teams can cooperate enough so they each get 30 points.
➤ Make it a bit easier by allowing them to talk throughout the game.

CHAPTER 6

Coping: Dealing with Change

CHANGE TIME LINE

This is . . .   An activity in which participants learn from major changes they have worked through.

The purpose is . . .   Participants see that, even when changes seem to create problems, they can find ways to overcome and be successful. They will also get to know each other a little better.

Use this when . . .
- ➤ The group is experiencing lots of change at work.
- ➤ The group lacks confidence to accomplish what is ahead of them.
- ➤ You don't have prep time and/or materials for anything more elaborate.

Materials you'll need . . .
- ➤ Paper and pens for each participant.

Here's how . . .
1. Give a pen and paper to each participant.
2. Have them each remember five major changes they have experienced in their lifetimes.
3. Participants draw time lines of their lives. Mark when each of the major changes occurred with an "X."
4. Have the participants pair up.
5. Ask them to share with their partner one of the major changes.

6. Post these questions for them to answer as they share:
   a. What made the change difficult?
   b. What was the key to your success in dealing with the change?
   c. How did you feel before, during, and after the change?
   d. How were the other changes going on around that time (refer to the time line) affecting your ability to deal with this one?

Ask these questions . . .

➤ How did you feel sharing these experiences with each other? *(I felt a sense of closeness; I realized we have more in common; Empathy; etc.)*

➤ What did you learn from how your partner dealt with their major change?

➤ What did you learn about the compounding effect of changes that are close to each other? *(Alone they would be manageable, but together, they seemed overwhelming; The way to deal with one adversely affected the next one; etc.)*

➤ What implications does this have for us back on the job?

Tips for success . . .

➤ Tell the participants that they will be asked to share only one of the major life changes they remember, not all of them. Share only what is comfortable.

Try these variations . . .

➤ After the participants share their experiences, have them pair up with someone else and repeat the activity.

➤ Have the participants share their experiences in teams of three to six. This takes longer, but it will allow them to hear and learn from more experiences than just one or two.

➤ You may eliminate the time line (and the need for pens and paper). Just have the participants select a major change they have experienced, and then have the dialogue.

GUESS AND SWITCH

This is . . .   A guessing game in which participants switch teams often.

The purpose is . . .   Participants get comfortable with constantly changing teams and allegiances; also they will see how ineffective yes/no questions are.

Use this when . . .
- ➤ The makeup of the group is changing frequently.
- ➤ Individuals rely too much on close-ended questions.
- ➤ You don't have prep time and/or materials for anything more elaborate.

Materials you'll need . . .
- ➤ No materials are necessary for this activity.

Here's how . . .
1. Divide the group in half. The teams gather in opposite corners of the room.
2. One participant from each team leaves the room. Together, their task is to pick quickly any object in the world.
3. They return to the team opposite the one they left.
4. Each team then asks the participant questions to determine what the object is. They may ask only questions that can be answered with "yes" or "no."

5. When a team guesses the object, they clap their hands to win the round.
6. Both participants, who originally left the room, now join the winning team.
7. Each team selects a new participant to leave the room for another round.
8. Play continues until one team captures all members or until a predetermined time limit is reached.

For example . . . The object can be anything—a rake, an iron, a roller coaster, sand, baby oil, a cheetah, a rose, and so forth.

Ask these questions . . .
- ➤ How did you feel when your team started dwindling? *(Nervous, threatened, more competitive, frustrated, etc.)*
- ➤ How did you feel as your team started to grow? *(Excited and energized, superior, confident, glad to be part of a winning team, etc.)*
- ➤ How did you feel when you had to join a different team? *(Reluctant, not welcome, excited to be on the winning team, etc.)*
- ➤ Did you find a pattern of questioning emerge that proved successful for the team?
- ➤ What kinds of questions could we have asked to guess the object quicker? *(How is this object used? What is the object's size and shape? And other open-ended questions.)*
- ➤ What implications does this activity have for us back on the job?

Tips for success . . .
- ➤ Do not let the teams spend much time in selecting the participant who goes outside. Keep the game moving; make it quick.
- ➤ Questions must be answered quietly, or the other team will overhear and get clues.

Try these
variations . . .

➤ Make the guessing (and thus the rounds) go faster by limiting the object to a category (movie titles, gardening supplies, your organization's products or services, driving a car, etc.) or people (living or dead).

➤ If the group is large (more than 24 people), divide them into three or four teams in various corners. After participants from each group come back into the room, have them return to a different team than the one they left.

➤ Instead of asking questions to guess the object, have the participants act it out (like charades), or draw it on a board (like Pictionary®).

INDEX TOWERS

This is . . .	A building activity in which participants use index cards to create a tower.
The purpose is . . .	The group can find creative ways to overcome adversity and be successful, even when changes seem to create problems.
Use this when . . .	➤ The group is experiencing lots of change at work. ➤ Individuals need to be creative about finding efficiencies despite constant change. ➤ Individuals would benefit from a shot of competitiveness.
Materials you'll need . . .	➤ A yardstick or tape measure. ➤ 50 index cards for each team. ➤ A roll of tape for each team. ➤ Small prizes for the winning team (optional).
Here's how . . .	1. Divide the group into teams of three to five. 2. Give each team 25 index cards and a roll of tape. 3. Each team has 5 minutes to build the tallest free-standing structure possible, using only the materials provided. 4. The structure must stand long enough for you to measure it. 5. After you measure all structures, have the teams destroy them. 6. Announce that you have found that the tape violates health laws and must be forfeited.

7. Now give each team 25 more index cards.
8. Each team has 5 minutes to build the tallest free-standing structure using only the materials provided (the 25 new index cards).
9. Measure the structures and determine the tallest.

Ask these questions . . .

➤ How did you decide on the structure to build each time?
➤ How did you feel when I removed the tape? *(Despair, challenged, frustrated, etc.)*
➤ What ways did you find to be successful in the second round? *(Cooperated more, found better ways to stack the cards, etc.)*
➤ What implications does this activity have for us back on the job?

Tips for success . . .

➤ Most teams will find a way to build an even taller structure without the tape. If they do not, ask if they think that eventually they could do so (given more time to practice or strategize).
➤ Colored index cards invite the team to aim for aesthetics as well as function.
➤ Be very careful approaching the structures to measure. You don't want to create a slight draft that topples their hard work!

Try these variations . . .

➤ Start with staplers instead of tape.
➤ When you take the tape away, replace it with staplers for round 2. Sometimes it is not so obvious whether change is good or bad.
➤ Have a third round in which you increase the number of index cards given to the teams or include some larger index cards. Some change is actually good.
➤ Make the activity go faster by reducing the number of index cards you distribute and then by reducing the time you give them to work.

MACHINES

This is . . .	An activity in which participants create a human machine and then have to change the machine per the customer's request.
The purpose is . . .	Participants learn that changes can create opportunity for improvement.
Use this when . . .	➤ The group is experiencing lots of change at work. ➤ Individuals need to be creative about finding solutions during change. ➤ You don't have prep time and/or materials for anything more elaborate.
Materials you'll need . . .	➤ No materials are necessary for this activity.
Here's how . . .	1. Divide the group into teams of 6–10. 2. Give each team 6 minutes to plan a human machine. All participants must be a part of this machine. 3. Watch each team demonstrate its machine 4. Then, select a participant from each machine. Announce that these "machine pieces" are obsolete. 5. The teams now have 3 more minutes to adjust or reinvent their machines using their selected participant in a new way.
Ask these questions . . .	➤ How did you decide on the machine design? ➤ How did you handle disagreements in the team?

> How did you feel when I rejected your original design? *(Frustrated and angry with you, hurt that you singled me out, anxious to improve the design, etc.)*

> How do we typically react to changes in our own work environment?

> What implications does this have for us back on the job?

Tips for success . . .

> Encourage the teams to be highly creative in their efforts, to use sound effects, and so forth.

> When selecting the participant who will be obsolete, choose the one who has the most pivotal role in the machine. This will force the team to really work on redesigning it.

> Give a 1-minute warning before time is up.

Try these variations . . .

> Impose a purpose or use for the machine, so the teams are then in competition with each other for the best machine for that purpose.

> Require that the planning, assembly, and demonstration be done without speaking.

> After the first machines have been demonstrated, have the teams find a way to incorporate all their machines into one giant machine. This will take the emphasis off of change and place it on creative teamwork and cooperation.

> Have some unusual props available. Assign one or more props to each team. Have them incorporate the prop into their machine design from the beginning or halfway through the activity. Props could include an eggbeater, a broom, a watering can, a silk flower, and so forth.

MAKEOVERS

This is . . . An activity in which participants cut up a picture and then rearrange the pieces into a new image.

The purpose is . . . Participants see how new and good things can come from changing what was.

Use this when . . .
- ➤ The group is experiencing lots of change at work.
- ➤ Individuals need to be creative about finding solutions during change.
- ➤ Individuals are seeing only the negative aspects of change.

Materials you'll need . . .
- ➤ At least one picture from a magazine for each participant.
- ➤ Scissors and glue stick for each participant.
- ➤ A piece of flipchart paper or other paper for the base of the new picture.

Here's how . . .
1. Allow each participant to select one picture.
2. Have her cut her picture into small pieces. The pieces should be small enough that the original picture is no longer evident.
3. Each participant uses his or her own pieces to create a new picture. Glue the pieces into a collage on flipchart paper.
4. After 10 minutes, have each participant share his collage and tell what it was before he changed it.

Ask these questions . . .
- ➤ How did you determine what collage to create?
- ➤ How did you feel when I gave you the assignment

to create a collage? *(Nervous, because I'm not creative; Anxious to get started; Worried mine might not be good; etc.)*

➤ How do these feeling compare to feelings we have when faced with change at work?

➤ What was the key to your finishing the task successfully?

➤ What implications does this have for us back on the job?

Tips for success . . .

➤ Have an assortment of pictures. The larger the pictures, the better.

➤ Do not give any ideas on what collage to create. They may struggle, but their own ideas will work better for them than any suggestion you may have.

➤ Give a 1-minute warning before the end of time.

Try these variations . . .

➤ Rather than magazine pictures, begin with headlines or other bold words. Have the participants cut the letters up and create a new message with their letters. Or use longer phrases: rather than cutting up letters, cut the words, and rearrange them, much like a ransom note might look!

➤ You can assign a specific theme for the collages such as dealing with change, teamwork, listening skills, quality, and so forth.

1, 2, 3, 4... NUMBERS

This is . . .   A fast paced number game in which participants either call numbers out quickly, or they are sent to the end of the line.

The purpose is . . .   Participants learn to cope with rapid-paced changes.

Use this when . . .
- ➤ The group is experiencing lots of change at work.
- ➤ Individuals need to see that minor mistakes are just that: minor!
- ➤ You don't have prep time and/or materials for anything more elaborate.

Materials you'll need . . .
- ➤ No materials are necessary for this activity.

Here's how . . .
1. Arrange the group into a "U" formation.
2. Have them count off down the line so everyone has a number.
3. The first participant begins by calling anyone else's number.
4. Immediately that person must call someone else's number.
5. Play continues like this until someone hesitates or calls an incorrect number (either their own number or a number that is not in the group).

6. That participant goes to the end of the line. She and everyone who was behind her now have a new number.

7. Resume play.

Ask these questions . . .

➤ How did you feel when you make a mistake? *(Like a failure, I let the team down, disappointed in myself, embarrassed, etc.)*

➤ How did it feel to watch someone else make a mistake? *(Empathy, glad it wasn't me, angry or frustrated, disappointed, etc.)*

➤ What is our typical reaction when we make minor mistakes at work? (Point out that changes lead to some minor mistakes, and we should not focus on them.)

➤ How did you feel as your number kept changing? How did you feel watching the pressure others were experiencing, but you weren't?

➤ What implications does this have for us on the job?

Tips for success . . .

➤ Have the group set a pace by clapping hands to a beat.

➤ Quicken the pace so everyone "fails" often and the numbers change frequently.

➤ Watch to see if anyone tries deliberately to trip up those at the beginning of the line. Ask why during the Debrief. Do we not like to see others remain successful?

Try these variations . . .

➤ When a participant makes a mistake, encourage him or her to take a bow, and have the group applaud him or her. Reinforce the concept that learning from minor mistakes is truly a good thing!

➤ Use the alphabet instead of numbers.

PUZZLED THUMBS

This is . . .   A puzzle activity in which the rules for puzzle assembly change halfway through the exercise.

The purpose is . . .   Participants will experience the value that information has when dealing with change. They will also see that their own reactions to change are normal and manageable.

Use this when . . .
➤ The group is experiencing lots of change at work.
➤ Individuals need to be creative about finding efficiencies despite constant change.
➤ Individuals need to understand that most reactions to change are normal and often take time to work through.
➤ The group is resisting change.

Materials you'll need . . .
➤ One children's puzzle for each small group. The best puzzles have a solid frame and border with 15–25 pieces.
➤ A stopwatch, watch, or clock with a second hand.

Here's how . . .
1. Divide the group into smaller teams of two to four.
2. Give each team a puzzle. Have them separate all the pieces and place them face up on the table. No puzzle piece may be touching any other puzzle piece to begin.
3. Time the teams assembling their puzzles.
4. Repeat the puzzle assembly two more times; the teams should try to improve their assembly time.

5. Now, inform them that thumbs may no longer be used. Each time a thumb touches a puzzle piece, 1 minute is added to that team's final time.
6. Time the teams assembling their puzzles.
7. Repeat the puzzle assembly two more times; the teams should try to improve their assembly time.
8. After six rounds, compare times and discuss.

Ask these questions . . .

➤ How did you feel about the first three rounds? *(Energized, excited, competitive, foolish making children's puzzles at work, etc.)*
➤ How did you feel about your last three rounds? *(Less excited, angry with you for prohibiting thumbs, discouraged, frustrated with our slower times, etc.)*
➤ How did you react when I told you that you couldn't use your thumbs any more? *(Excited about the challenge, demotivated, discouraged, angry, etc.)*
➤ What if I had explained that you couldn't use your thumbs because we discovered a carcinogen on the puzzle pieces that affected humans ONLY when it touched their thumbs? *(I'd be less angry, happy you're watching out for us, angry we had already been exposed, etc.)*
➤ How does having information about changes help you cope at work?
➤ What could have been done to make the last three rounds more productive for you? *(Watch for whether the group focuses on what they could do/control or what you could do/control, pliers or other new tools, etc.)*
➤ What implications does this have back on the job?

Tips for success . . .

➤ As you watch the clock, call out times as the teams finish. They can record their own times. Or, have each team time themselves with the second hands on their own watches.

➤ After you announce the thumb rule, listen to their comments. They will often say things such as, "What a stupid rule. This is going to slow us down. . ." These remarks make for great discussion afterwards!

Try these variations . . .

➤ Tell half the groups the reason for Thumbs Rule and the other half not. Compare the differences in attitudes and times between these groups.

➤ For competitive groups, keep a running record of best times on a flipchart or board.

➤ The task can be something other than puzzles—towers of plastic building blocks, house of cards, lines of dominoes, and so forth.

➤ Make it more team-focused by recording only the time of the slowest team. The teams will learn to share best practices with each other to better everyone's times.

➤ Switch puzzles after the first three rounds.

➤ After six rounds, remove the puzzle frame for another three rounds (still not allowing thumbs), or blindfold the participants. These more difficult changes will simulate the feeling of constant change that many feel at work. Afterwards, discuss how the changes compounded reactions. What can be done to minimize the negative impact of that phenomenon?

➤ Blindfold only one person on each team, but allow only that person to still use his or her thumbs. How did the teams work around the blindness and leverage the available thumbs?

SIMON SEZ

This is . . .	A Simon Says activity that twists the rules for play.
The purpose is . . .	Participants learn to listen to instructions and pay attention to changed rules.
Use this when . . .	➤ The group is experiencing lots of change at work. ➤ Individuals are not listening well. ➤ You don't have prep time and/or materials for anything more elaborate.
Materials you'll need . . .	➤ No materials are necessary for this activity.
Here's how . . .	1. Select someone to be Simon. Everyone else stands facing him. 2. Simon calls out simple commands. 3. If the command begins with "Simon says. . ." participants must *not* obey, or they are eliminated from play. 4. If the command does not begin with "Simon says. . ." participants *must* obey the command, or they are eliminated from play. 5. Simon tries to eliminate everyone from play. 6. Repeat with a new Simon if time allows.
For example . . .	"Lift one foot." (Everyone does it.) "Simon says scratch your eyebrow." (No one does it.) "Touch your nose." (Everyone does it.) "Raise your right hand." (Everyone does it.)

Ask these questions . . .	➤ How did it feel to play this children's game backwards? *(It was confusing, easy, harder to concentrate on the opposite of what I knew, etc.)*
	➤ How did you feel when you were eliminated? *(Defeated, glad to have the pressure off, angry with myself for messing up, etc.)*
	➤ What rules (policies) have we turned upside down here lately?
	➤ How hard was it for Simon to give directions differently? How does this compare to a manager caught up in change at work? *(It may be just as hard for him or her to adjust as the rest of us; He or she may be resistant; He or she may make mistakes; etc.)*
	➤ What implications does this have for us back on the job?
Tips for success . . .	➤ Encourage Simon to do the action as he's commanding them, whether he says, "Simon says. . ." or not. Many participants get locked into following the visual clue, not the verbal cue.
	➤ Even if a participant just makes a start to do as "Simon says," they are eliminated.
Try these variations . . .	➤ Just for fun, replace "Simon" with the name of your organization's president or CEO.
	➤ Have two Simon's up there alternating commands with or without "Simon says. . .", working together to eliminate participants. How did listening to two people give commands affect the staying power of the participants?
	➤ More difficult? Have two Simons. One is obeyed only when he says, "Simon says," and the other is obeyed only when she does not say, "Simon says."

WRONG-HANDED PICTURE

This is . . .   A drawing activity in which participants use the hand they normally do not use for writing.

The purpose is . . .   Participants get a sense of how they react to change and learn that their own reactions to change are typical or normal.

Use this when . . .
- ➤ The group is experiencing lots of change at work.
- ➤ Individuals need to understand that most reactions to change are normal and often take time to work through.
- ➤ You don't have prep time and/or materials for anything more elaborate.

Materials you'll need . . .
- ➤ Paper and pens for each participant.

Here's how . . .
1. Give a pen and paper to each participant.
2. Give the participants 6 minutes to draw a picture of something in their office or workspace.
3. Participants must draw this object with the hand they normally do not use for writing.
4. Have the participants exchange their pictures with someone else.
5. This participant will label the picture according to what they think it is and give it back to its artist.

Ask these questions . . .	➤ How many objects were guessed correctly?
	➤ How did it feel to use your other hand? *(Awkward, confusing, not that bad, etc.)*
	➤ How did those feelings affect your picture? *(Made it more shaky; I put less into it; etc.)*
	➤ How did you work through those feelings? *(Sheer determination; I asked for help; reassured myself; etc.)*
	➤ How do those feelings compare with the feelings we have regarding the changes we are experiencing?
	➤ What implications does this have for us back on the job?

Tips for success . . .	➤ Post the pictures around the break room, conference room, or lunchroom, so participants can refer to them and be reminded of what they learned from this activity.
	➤ Take the emphasis off artwork, so participants do not shy away from drawing.
	➤ For participants who are adamant about not drawing, have them write a sentence or two describing the object. The crooked handwriting will be just as much a catalyst for learning as the drawing would have been.
	➤ Give a 1-minute warning before time is up.

Try these variations . . .	➤ Use colored markers or colored pencils to add an element of creativity to the activity.
	➤ Make this more difficult by having them draw one of the changes currently happening at work that is affecting them.
	➤ Rather than draw the object, have the participants write a sentence or two describing it.
	➤ Have the participants pair up. Take turns describing an object to a partner so that he can draw it with his other hand. This variation will focus on communication skills as well as dealing with change.

CHAPTER 7

Creativity: Solving Problems Together

SEVEN HANDS

This is . . . An activity in which participants solve an ancient stacking puzzle.

The purpose is . . . Participants learn how to work together toward a solution.

Use this when . . .
- ➤ The group has difficulty dealing with conflict over processes or methods.
- ➤ Individuals are impatient with delays that keep them from moving forward quickly.
- ➤ Individuals need help seeing patterns emerge in problems.

Materials you'll need . . .
- ➤ Washable ink marker or pens.
- ➤ Three sheets of paper for each team.

Here's how . . .
1. Divide the group into teams of four to seven.
2. In each team, all participants mark the backs of their hands with a number from 1 to 7 (if the team has fewer than seven participants, some may have to mark both hands).
3. Lay three pieces of paper in front of each team.
4. Participants stack their hands on one paper in order from "7" on the bottom to "1" on the top. This is the "start" position.

5. Each team is to restack their hands in the exact same order (with "7" on the bottom) using only these moves:
   a. Move only one hand at a time.
   b. Move a hand onto another hand (or stack of hands) or onto an empty paper.
   c. Move only the top hand on a stack.
   d. Never move a hand on top of a lower numbered hand.

For example . . . "3" can never be placed on top of "1" or "2."
"3" can be placed on top of "4" or "5" or "6" or "7" or an empty paper.
"5" cannot be placed on top of "1" or "2" or "3" or "4."
"5" cannot be pulled out from under any number of hands; it can be moved only when it is on top.

Ask these questions . . .
➤ What strategy did you use to be successful?
➤ How were differences of opinion about how to move handled in your team?
➤ Did you have a leader? How was he or she selected?
➤ When someone on your team thought he or she knew the solution or at least the next move, how did he or she behave? How did you respond to that?
➤ Did you ever feel like you were backtracking? How did that make you feel? *(Frustrated, like we were wasting time, we had messed up, etc.)*
➤ When do we backtrack to move forward in our organization?
➤ What implications does this have for us back on the job?

Tips for success . . .
➤ This solution can be accomplished in 127 moves.
➤ You can get a sense for the solution by trying the

puzzle ahead of time. Label seven index cards and stack them according to the instructions above. Start solving!

➤ Watch and listen to comments made during the activity. Bring up relevant ones during the Debrief.

➤ Use this opportunity to mix participants up. Arrange teams so that participants who do not normally work together are on the same team.

Try these
variations . . .

➤ If you have less time, use only five (easy) or six (moderate) hands instead of seven.

➤ Use blocks or some other objects. The dynamics change considerably when the participants are not touching each other. If you have several teams, some may use hands, some blocks. Compare their responses to the Debrief questions.

BALLOON SCULPTURES

This is . . . A fun activity in which participants create a balloon sculpture that reflects the team.

The purpose is . . . The group members openly express their commitment to the team.

Use this when . . .
- ➤ A new team is forming and needs to come together.
- ➤ Creative thinking is not happening very much.
- ➤ Individuals are not cooperating well.
- ➤ The group needs a shot in the arm of team spirit.

Materials you'll need . . .
- ➤ One long balloon (the kind circus clowns use) for each participant and some extras.
- ➤ A balloon pump (optional but highly recommended, often included with the purchase of the balloons).

Here's how . . .
1. Give each participant one balloon.
2. Have the entire team create a balloon structure that reflects their commitment to the team.

For example . . . Balloons linked together may suggest interdependence, balloons touching may represent connectivity, balloons on the bottom may suggest supporting others, and so forth.

Ask these questions . . .
- ➤ How does this activity relate to teamwork? *(We had to work together; We had to agree on things;*

We had to support the final outcome; Each balloon reflected our individual input; etc.)

➤ How did you deal with everyone's ideas about the sculpture?

➤ How did you handle disagreements?

➤ What implication does this have for us back on the job?

Tips for success . . .

➤ Have the balloons blown up before the activity if possible.

➤ Have extra balloons ready for the few that will break.

➤ Do not blow the balloons up completely. Leave an inch or more to allow for bending and stretching.

➤ Watch for team behaviors during the activity that you can bring up during the Debrief.

Try these variations . . .

➤ If the group consists of intact work teams, divide the group into those teams. Have them each create a sculpture. Then have them share their creation with the others. If there are fewer than five participants in a team, you may need to make more balloons available for them.

➤ Have the team think of a team name that complements their sculpture and reinforces their commitment to the team.

➤ Use building blocks instead of balloons. Give each participant five or more blocks.

➤ Instead of balloons, use your organization's own products or items to which your group can particularly relate.

CARD STACK

This is . . .	An activity in which participants organize a random stack of cards into the best arrangement possible.
The purpose is . . .	Participants learn to cooperate with each other, have fun, and reinforce communication skills.
Use this when . . .	➤ Individuals need to understand the value of being flexible with plans and strategies. ➤ Creative problem solving is not happening very much. ➤ Individuals are not cooperating well.
Materials you'll need . . .	➤ A set of 16 random playing cards for each team.

Here's how . . .	1. Divide the group into teams of three to five.
	2. Give each team a set of 16 playing cards.
	3. Have the teams lay out all their cards in a grid (four rows and four columns).
	4. The object is for them to reduce the 16 cards down to one stack, or the smallest number of stacks possible.
	5. Explain these rules:
	   a. A card (or stack) may be moved any distance horizontally or vertically, but never diagonally.
	   b. It must always end its move on top of another card (or stack) that is the same rank or suit. It can never take an empty space.

  c. Once a card is placed on top of another card, the resulting stack is moved as one unit driven by its top card (all cards below become irrelevant for the remainder of the game).

6. Allow the teams 10 minutes to play.

For example . . . A 2 of diamonds may move horizontally 1 space to cover a stack topped by a 4 of diamonds (matching suit) or vertically 3 spaces to cover a 2 of clubs (matching rank). (It cannot be moved diagonally for any reason.) Once the 2 is moved to cover the 4, that 4 becomes irrelevant. The new stack, consisting of the 2, the 4, and cards below the 4, is now moved as one unit based on the top card, the 2 of diamonds. Or, the reverse move could have been made. The stack topped with a 4 of diamonds could have been moved horizontally to cover the 2 of diamonds. The resulting stack, with the 2 of diamonds on the bottom, is now moved according to its top card, the 4 of diamonds.

Ask these questions . . .
- ➤ How close were you to the goal of one final stack?
- ➤ What affected your final result? Since each set of cards was different, how did available resources affect the outcome? Does this happen at work?
- ➤ How did you deal with everyone's ideas about the way to proceed?
- ➤ How does this activity relate to teamwork? *(We had to cooperate; We had to agree on a process; We had to listen to each other; etc.)*
- ➤ Did anyone emerge as the leader? How did he or she function?
- ➤ How did you handle disagreements?
- ➤ What implications does this have for us back on the job?

Tips for success . . .	➤ Post the rules so participants can refer to them during play.
	➤ Help the teams remember that once a card is on top of one or more other cards, that card stack moves as one unit. Only the top card remains relevant to play.
	➤ Stacks can move on top of other stacks to create a new stack. Again, only the top card remains relevant to play.
	➤ Play with a set of cards beforehand so you get a sense of the card movements.
Try these variations . . .	➤ Give the teams exactly the same set of 16 cards. Increase the competition by announcing the exact configuration of cards from which all teams begin play.
	➤ Use more cards for greater difficulty, fewer cards to finish in less time (but using fewer than 12 cards does not allow the team to grasp the learning points).
	➤ Allow one diagonal move per game. How does the added "flexibility" impact the final outcome? Not all change is bad!
	➤ Have the teams remember how they configured their cards the first time. Play another round, and see if they can improve their results. Add a level of change by having one participant from each team move to a different team for the second round. How did this new pair of eyes affect the results?

CONSULTANTS

This is . . . An activity that allows participants to give each other advice on how to handle work problems.

The purpose is . . . Participants get help solving problems or get creative ideas for dealing with work issues.

Use this when . . .
➤ Individuals are not helping or supporting each other very well.
➤ Individuals need to see the value of others' input and help.
➤ You don't have prep time and/or materials for anything more elaborate.

Materials you'll need . . .
➤ Paper and pens for each participant.

Here's how . . .
1. Each participant writes one problem or concern he or she currently faces at the top of a piece of paper. Give the group 2 minutes to do this.
2. Have everyone pass their papers to the participant on their left.
3. Each participant has 1 minute to read the problem in front of him or her and write some advice.
4. Pass the papers again, and repeat as often as time allows.
5. Return the papers to the original owners.

For example . . .

Problem:

➤ I have trouble making eye contact when giving negative feedback.

Solutions:

➤ Try practicing in a mirror.

➤ Make sure your feedback is not attacking or otherwise making the person feel defensive; then maybe it won't be so hard.

➤ Role-play with a friend.

➤ Remember, it may not be as negative as you fear it is!

➤ Watch how easily Jolene does it, she's a pro!

Ask these questions . . .

➤ How many got one or more ideas that will truly help them resolve their issue?

➤ How did you feel having to give advice? *(On the spot, at a loss, honored and respected, pressured to come up with something fantastic, etc.)*

➤ Why do we not ask each other for help more often? *(Do not want to impose, think we have to have the answer ourselves, do not trust others will have any good ideas, etc.)*

➤ What implications does this have for us back on the job?

Tips for success . . .

➤ Encourage partial advice. If a participant cannot think of advice, he or she can write a few words of encouragement and support or suggest another resource to go to for advice.

➤ The advice does not have to be revolutionary or complete. Usually the first thought that comes to mind is a good one. Even if it is not a very good one, it may prompt someone else to come up with a better one!

Try these
variations . . .

➤ Sit in a circle. The first participant explains briefly his or her problem or concern. All other participants take turns offering advice out loud. The first participant cannot say a word (to explain why something will not work, for example)—just listen and thank the others for their help.

➤ This activity can work for creative idea generation rather than problem solving. For example, where should we go for our holiday dinner, how can we increase community service participation, and so forth.

IMPROVE THIS

This is . . . A very quick activity in which participants try to improve their seating arrangement with no specific goal in mind.

The purpose is . . . Participants learn that objectives or goals must be specific; that assumptions left unchecked can sabotage an effort.

Use this when . . .
- ➤ Individuals need to see the value of setting clear and specific goals.
- ➤ Individuals are making assumptions or not asking questions for clarification.
- ➤ You don't have prep time and/or materials for anything more elaborate.

Materials you'll need . . .
- ➤ No materials are necessary for this activity.

Here's how . . .
1. Announce to the group that they have exactly 60 seconds to improve their seating arrangement.
2. Do not give any further instruction. Look at a clock and tell them to begin . . . now!
3. If they ask for clarification, simply repeat the original instructions.
4. Stop the activity after 60 seconds and discuss.

Ask these questions . . .
- ➤ Did you meet your objective? *(Yes, because I am closer to the window; No, because I'm not sure what the objective was; I'm not sure. . .)*

> What was your objective? Was it clear? (If they think it was clear, ask them to define "improve," and then show how it could have meant to get more people up front, or to get in a better circle, or to sit boy–girl–boy–girl, etc., to show there were assumptions made.)
> Did you seek clarification? Why not? Or what happened when you tried?
> How does this situation relate to the workplace? *(We often try to accomplish things when we are not clear on the real goal or the specific criteria for success; We often don't ask for clarification, and if we do, we don't press until we get what we truly need to succeed; etc.)*
> What can we do to prevent this kind of thing happening back on the job?

Tips for success . . .

> After giving the instructions, do not ask if there are any questions. Look at the clock to discourage their questions. It is amazing how quickly anyone wanting clarification will back off if the source appears elusive. Usually, the pressure of the group will discourage anyone from not moving quickly.
> If they directly ask for clarification, say, *"You determine for yourselves what "improve" means. You are all adults. It seems pretty obvious."* During the Debrief, point out how similar this is to responses back on the job.
> Do not be surprised (and do not stop them!) if they start moving tables and chairs to "improve" their seating arrangement.
> During the Debrief, do not beat them up for their behavior. Remember, you set them up. The purpose is to show them how often their work environment sets them up like this, and how they typically respond.

> As they rearrange themselves, listen to their comments. They will say things such as, *"I don't know what she wants, but let's try this. . ."* Bring these up (without pointing at who said what) during the Debrief.

Try these variations . . .

> This does not have to be done at the beginning of a meeting. Done at any other time, it can also energize the group that is lagging a bit.

> For more focused and in-depth learning, you can give them a specific work goal and have them improve it. For example, *Improve order processing* is vague, as stated; improving it will be difficult without getting clarity about successful customer service. *Be more helpful to customers* is equally vague.

> After doing this activity as outlined, try variations wherein you are explicit about what you want them to accomplish, and see how closely the group meets your expectations. Let others take a turn being specific with the goal.

ONE-WORDED STORIES

This is . . . A story telling activity in which participants construct a story together by contributing one word at a time.

The purpose is . . . Participants practice cooperating and making each other look good.

Use this when . . .
➤ Individuals are not cooperating well.
➤ Individuals are focusing too much on themselves.
➤ You don't have prep time and/or materials for anything more elaborate.

Materials you'll need . . .
➤ No materials are necessary for this activity.

Here's how . . .
1. Explain that the group will create a story together, one word at a time.
2. The word used must be as interesting as possible, and it must make the word of the preceding participant work as well as possible.
3. Select one participant to demonstrate how "Once upon a time. . ." might come out with each of you alternating saying those words.
4. After the story is over, try another one or two (the group will get better at this).

For	Participant 1: "Once"
example . . .	Participant 2: "upon"
	Participant 3: "a"
	Participant 4: "time"
	Participant 5: "my"
	Participant 6: "uncle"
	Participant 7: "and"
	Participant 8: "his"
	Participant 9: "ugly. . ."

Ask these	➤ How many felt the person after you said the
questions . . .	"wrong" word, because that was not what you meant to have come out? How did that make you feel? *(Angry, frustrated, critical, etc.)*
	➤ How would you compare the collective story of the group with what you may have come up with on your own? *(It was more creative and original; It made less sense; It was more fun; etc.)*
	➤ Who did not like where the story went? Why not? What could you have done had this been a work situation?
	➤ Which story was the best? Why?
	➤ What implications does this have for us back on the job, especially when someone does not understand what you intended?

Tips for	➤ Keep the pace moving along quickly, or the flow
success . . .	of story will be lost repeatedly.
	➤ End the story when it feels like it has run its course, or the energy and enthusiasm for that one has waned.
	➤ Encourage participants to speak loudly and very clearly.

Try these	➤ To keep the story moving, allow participants the
variations . . .	option of pointing to the next person when they

want to pass. Afterwards, ask how the group felt about those who passed. Did anyone pass more than others? How does the group interpret that behavior? Are there some who "pass" at work more often than others?

➤ To encourage teamwork, allow other participants to offer to take someone's turn if they hesitate. Afterwards, ask the how the group felt about those who offered help. Did anyone hesitate more than others? Did anyone jump to the rescue more than others?

➤ Use paper. Have each participant start a poem with one line. Pass to the left. Add a line that rhymes. Pass to the left four more times. Read the poems out loud.

➤ Don't take turns at all. Let whoever wants to add a word do so. Did someone dominate? Did anyone not participate?

PAPER SHUFFLE

This is . . . An activity in which participants put a newspaper in numerical or page order after it has been shuffled.

The purpose is . . . Participants learn to cooperate with each other, have fun, and reinforce communication skills.

Use this when . . .
- ➤ Individuals are not cooperating well.
- ➤ A new group is forming and needs to come together.
- ➤ The group needs to loosen up, have some fun, and laugh.

Materials you'll need . . .
- ➤ One newspaper with all pages completely shuffled and out of order for each team.
- ➤ Small prizes for the winning team (optional).

Here's how . . .
1. Divide the group into teams of four to six participants.
2. Give each team one newspaper, completely shuffled.
3. Have the team sort and reorganize the newspaper back into its original order.

Ask these questions . . .
- ➤ How does this activity relate to teamwork? *(We had to cooperate; We had to agree on a process; We had to listen to each other; etc.)*
- ➤ How did you deal with everyone's ideas about the way to proceed?
- ➤ Did anyone emerge as the leader? How did he or she function?
- ➤ How did you handle disagreements?

> What implications does this have for us back on the job?

Tips for success . . .
> Use an identical newspaper for each team. If you use other materials, make sure the number of pages given to each team is equal.
> Do not give any suggestions or advice before or during the task. Let the team members figure things out for themselves.

Try these variations . . .
> Use pages ripped from an old book, but cut off the page numbers first!
> Use a long document from your organization, such as a procedures manual.
> Do not allow the participants to speak during this activity.
> If the group is too small to form teams, time the group performing the task. Then reshuffle the paper and see if they can improve their time.
> A follow-up activity for fun and to build camaraderie is to have each team use their newspaper and some tape to create a costume for one of their teammates. The teams can compete for most original, most funny, most beautiful, and so forth.

CHAPTER 8

Z, Y, X, W, V... Teamwork: Appreciating and Supporting Each Other

BLAME GAME

This is . . .
A quick standstill activity in which participants try to determine who moved first and then assign blame.

The purpose is . . .
Participants see that everyone is responsible for group behavior.

Use this when . . .
- ➤ Individuals blame others for group problems that they also influence.
- ➤ Energy is being wasted finding culprits and scapegoats.
- ➤ You don't have prep time and/or materials for anything more elaborate.

Materials you'll need . . .
- ➤ No materials are necessary for this activity.

Here's how . . .
1. Arrange the group in a large circle, with everyone standing.
2. Find your Idol:
   a. You begin by pointing to someone in the circle. Keep pointing.
   b. That participant now points to someone else and keeps pointing.
   c. Continue until everyone is pointing at someone else, and the last participant then points at you.

d. Stop pointing (drop your hands) and fix your eyes on the participant you were pointing at. That participant becomes your Idol.

3. Explain that the objective is to watch your Idol closely and copy his or her every action.

4. Now ask the group to stand perfectly still. No one may move *unless* his or her Idol does. And if his or her Idol moves (twitches, coughs, blinks, etc.), he or she is to mimic that movement exactly and then be still again.

5. Begin the game and play for several minutes.

Ask these questions . . .

➤ We were supposed to stand still—what happened? (Expect some participants immediately to start blaming their Idol for moving.)

➤ Who knows who started the movement? (Allow for some accusations; inevitably it will be difficult or impossible to pinpoint who really started each movement.)

➤ How much does it matter who started it, once it got started?

➤ How much energy do we spend looking for scapegoats?

➤ How are we to blame for perpetuating certain behaviors that eventually become team norms? What examples of this do we have here at work?

➤ What implications does this have for us back on the job?

Tips for success . . .

➤ Small movements are bound to happen. When they do, the movement will be duplicated around the group endlessly. Usually it will be exaggerated.

➤ If the movement gets out of hand, just stop the game, refocus everyone, and start again.

Try these variations . . .

➤ Designate one participant as "where the buck stops." When movement starts and moves around the group, that participant will NOT repeat it. This variation is effective after a few rounds of the regular activity. Ask how much influence one person can have in affecting team behavior.

BUT NOTHING (FEEDBACK)

This is . . .   A quick verbal activity in which participants give each other personal feedback using "but. . ."

The purpose is . . .   Participants learn how easily "but. . ." can interfere with constructive feedback by creating defensiveness, even when they mean well. They will also learn to replace "but. . ." with "and. . ."

Use this when . . .
- Feedback is not being received very well.
- Individuals feel like others are not listening with open minds.
- You don't have prep time and/or materials for anything more elaborate.

Materials you'll need . . .
- No materials are necessary for this activity.

Here's how . . .
1. Have the participants pair up.
2. Each participant has 30 seconds to think of something she likes about the other's outfit and one way the outfit could be improved.
3. The first participant tells the other what she likes first, then says, "but. . ." and finishes the sentence with how it could be even better.
4. The other participant then does the same to the first participant.

5. Now have each participant repeat what she just said, replacing "but" with "and."

For example . . .
"I like that tie, but it would bring out your blue eyes better if it was red."
"I like that tie, and it would bring out your blue eyes better if it was red."
"That is a nice dress, but you would look even more professional if you had earrings, too."
"That is a nice dress, and you would look even more professional if you had earrings, too."

Ask these questions . . .
➤ How did it feel to hear "but?" *(Annoying, defensive, insincere, etc.)* How did it feel to hear "and?" *(Helped, respected, supported, etc.)*
➤ What does "but" usually mean? *(Disregard what you just heard, because here is the real truth.)*
➤ Why do we say "but" so often when giving suggestions or feedback?
➤ What implications does this have for us back on the job?

Tips for success . . .
➤ Share an example to give participants a sense of how the statements should sound.
➤ Make sure all pairs have finished their "but" statements before giving the cue to make the "and" statements.
➤ Point out that the word "but" usually negates everything that precedes it.

Try these variations . . .
➤ The more personal the feedback, the better. If the group is uncomfortable giving feedback on each other's outfits, though, select something else, such as the coffee in the lunchroom, a movie they have both seen, and so forth.

- ➤ After the meeting, ask for feedback on the meeting without the "but." *(I liked that we had an agenda,* and *next time I hope we can stick to it better.)*
- ➤ If the group is comfortable giving feedback to each other already, have them do it on their recent job performance rather than their outfit.
- ➤ Add an element of fun to this activity by starting with participants making something creatively (with clay, markers, balloons, building blocks, etc.), and then give the feedback to each other about the creation rather then their outfits.

BUT NOTHING (IDEAS)

This is . . .	A quick, verbal activity in which participants give each other feedback on their ideas using "yes, but. . ."
The purpose is . . .	Participants learn how easily "yes, but. . ." can shut down communication and creativity, even if well intentioned. They will also learn to replace "yes, but. . ." with "yes, and. . ."
Use this when . . .	➤ Ideas are being shot down frequently; creativity is being stifled. ➤ Individuals feel like others are not listening with open minds. ➤ You don't have prep time and/or materials for anything more elaborate.
Materials you'll need . . .	➤ No materials are necessary for this activity.
Here's how . . .	1. Have the participants pair up. 2. Each pair is to plan a vacation together (money is no object). 3. One partner starts by suggesting something to the other. 4. The other responds by saying, "Yes, but. . ." and finishes her sentence.

5. The first partner then responds by saying, "Yes, but. . ." and finishes her sentence.
6. The conversations continue back and forth this way for 2 minutes.
7. Then, have the same pairs do the same thing with only one change—each sentence must begin with "Yes, and. . ."
8. The conversations continue this way for 2 minutes.

For example . . .

"I want to go someplace warm."
"Yes, but let's make sure it's not Florida."
"Yes, but Puerto Rico could be nice."
"Yes, but I hope one of us speaks Spanish."
"Yes, but we could bring a dictionary, if necessary."
"I want to go someplace warm."
"Yes, and let's make sure it's not Florida."
"Yes, and St. Martin could be nice."
"Yes, and I hope one of us speaks French."
"Yes, and we could bring a dictionary, if necessary."

Ask these questions . . .

➤ How did it feel to hear "but?" *(Annoying, defensive, competitive, etc.)* And how did it feel to hear "and?" *(Accepted, listened to, respected, etc.)*
➤ Did you get along further with your plans during the first or second round? Why?
➤ Why do we say "yes, but. . ." so often? *(It is ingrained in us; The "but" allows us to disagree without being disagreeable; etc.)*
➤ When is "yes, but. . ." useful or appropriate?
➤ What implication does this have for us back on the job?

Tips for success . . .

➤ Read the examples above to give participants a feel for how the conversation might go.
➤ Encourage them to keep the conversation moving. They are not planning a real vacation, so they do not have to be accurate, precise, or realistic.

➤ The second dialogue does not have to duplicate word for word the first dialogue.

Try these variations . . .
➤ Ask the Debrief questions after the first round of "buts" while the team's thoughts and feelings are still fresh.
➤ Plan a party, family reunion, or any other elaborate event that might be fun.
➤ Divide the participants into small groups instead of pairs. The "Yes, but. . ." conversation goes around the circle.

FIRST IMPRESSIONS

This is . . .   An activity in which participants determine their first impressions of people picked at random from magazines.

The purpose is . . .   Participants see how strong and important others' first impression of them can be.

Use this when . . .
- ➤ Individuals interact with customers a great deal.
- ➤ First impressions of the group are critical for their success.
- ➤ Individuals are resisting their uniforms or other aspects of "the look" you want.

Materials you'll need . . .
- ➤ One envelope for each team that contains four or five pictures of people from magazines. Avoid famous or recognizable people. Avoid settings and backgrounds that are not neutral.

Here's how . . .
1. Divide the group into teams of four to six.
2. Give each group an envelope containing pictures of various people.
3. They have 6 minutes to discuss their first impressions of the people based solely on what they see in the picture.
4. Have them report back to the larger group on one of the pictures to which their team felt the strongest first impression.

For example . . .	"This woman is probably a professional. Look at the way her head is held up high. She's probably assertive and very sure of herself. Oh, and check out that necklace. Doesn't it just scream "success"? "No, I think that necklace begs for attention! I agree she looks pretty assertive, though. She also seems to. . ."
Ask these questions . . .	➤ How easy was it to agree on your first impressions of these people? ➤ What were some of the reasons for disagreement? *(Different upbringing, different history with a certain kind of look, etc.)* ➤ What judgments are others making about us and the way we present ourselves? ➤ What implications does this have for us on the job?
Tips for success . . .	➤ Keep the Debrief away from discussing whether first impressions are fair or not. Accept that they happen, and focus on how you can leverage that fact for your organization. ➤ Collect the pictures from various magazines. Try for as eclectic a mix as possible for each envelope. ➤ Be sensitive to racial or gender biases in your group and the pictures. ➤ Give a 1-minute warning before discussions are to end.
Try these variations . . .	➤ You can focus the first impressions specifically on facial expressions, clothing, body language, or whatever else you want to emphasize. ➤ You could refocus the Debrief to make this discussion more about diversity—accepting others for who and what they are. After giving out the envelopes of pictures, ask the teams to decide which

one they would most want to have join their team, and which one they would least like to have join their team. Why?

➤ Have the teams "fix" each picture by identifying how they would improve the look of each one to make them ready to join their team. Focus the Debrief on what they learned from each other concerning how they feel the group should be presenting themselves.

➤ Ask what product or service each pictured person would be representing or selling.

JUNK TO JEWELS

This is . . .	An activity in which participants take work-related items and show how those reflect what each participant brings to the strength of the team.
The purpose is . . .	Participants appreciate their own and each others' contribution to the team's success.
Use this when . . .	➤ A significant project or work effort is beginning. ➤ Individuals are not feeling confident about their ability to get the job done. ➤ Individuals need to bond together.
Materials you'll need . . .	➤ An array of items commonly found in your work environment—paper clips, pens, erasers, calculators, coffee mugs, staplers, sticky notes, rubber bands, and so forth.
Here's how . . .	1. Have each participant select an item that best represents what he or she feels he or she has to contribute to the team's success. 2. Have each participant share with the group why she chose the object she did. 3. Give the team 5 minutes to now make a sculpture using their items. The final sculpture should show how the individual parts would come together to strengthen the team and ensure success.

For example . . .	"I chose a calculator because I tend to be very analytical. I like to find solutions. I get more from the search for the answer than I do from the glory of having found it." "I also chose the calculator, but for me, it is because I am very detail focused. Approximations and guesses are not good enough for me. So I will attend to the details for this group."
Ask these questions . . .	➤ Why is it that the same item meant different things to different people? ➤ What were you thinking as you tried to incorporate everything into a sculpture? *(I wasn't sure how the stapler could be included; I wanted the pen to be more central; Some were more concerned about the finished product than others; etc.)* ➤ What implications does this have for us back on the job?
Tips for success . . .	➤ If the group is large (more than 15 people), divide the group into teams that represent intact work groups. ➤ Have more than one of each item on the table so several participants can choose the same thing (for different reasons?). ➤ A formal Debrief may be unnecessary if you discuss as participants each share their strengths.
Try these variations . . .	➤ You can make this activity more personal by having the participants select the item that best reflects their personality, and then explain why. ➤ Make this a development activity. Have the participants select the item that best represents what they want to develop in themselves. Invite the others to support and assist them.

KUDOS

This is . . .	A recognition activity in which their peers, not their boss, appreciate the participants.
The purpose is . . .	Participants receive recognition and appreciation from each other and have it reinforced by the whole team.
Use this when . . .	➤ A significant project or work effort has been completed—to celebrate the success.
	➤ Individuals are feeling down or less confident about themselves.
	➤ Individuals need to recognize and appreciate what's going right among themselves.
	➤ Individuals need to bond together.
Materials you'll need . . .	➤ A box or two of Kudos® candy bars.
Here's how . . .	1. Show a box of Kudos® bars to the group, and make sure everyone knows what the word kudos means.
	2. Explain that they are to use the candy bars to recognize each other for things they have accomplished.
	3. Anyone can give anyone else a candy bar. They can give more than one, if they like.
	4. The only stipulation is that it must be accompanied by a brief and *specific* explanation of why.
	5. Do not go in any order. Do not require anyone to give a candy bar. Let this be entirely voluntary.

6. You go first. Give a Kudos® bar to a participant. As you do, explain what that person did to receive the bar.

7. Encourage the participants to follow your lead— someone (anyone) can now give a candy bar to someone else.

8. Initiate a short round of applause for the recipient after each award.

9. Continue until the enthusiasm dies down, or until you run out of candy bars.

For example . . . "Kudos to Vanessa for helping me research that billing error last Thursday. She helped me whittle down the possible causes for the error. I was able to get back to the customer with an answer much quicker than if I had worked on it by myself."

Ask these questions . . .
➤ How difficult (or easy) was it to give each other recognition? Why?
➤ How does recognition from your peers differ from recognition you get from me?
➤ What do you think would happen if we gave feedback like this to colleagues outside our group (vendors, internal clients, suppliers, customers, support staff, etc.)?

Tips for success . . .
➤ The first participant to give a candy bar may be tentative, but once the concept catches on, participants often start fighting over who gets to recognize whom next (and isn't that a wonderful "fight" to have?).
➤ The recipient of the candy bar is never expected to give one to someone else. Let whoever wants to give a candy bar give one. Do not worry about taking turns or going in order.

- ➤ You may want to tell one participant about the activity beforehand and ask him to be prepared to hand out a candy bar after you do, just to get the ball rolling.
- ➤ You can use this as a regular feature of your ongoing staff meetings. It never gets old, and the participants will never run out of things to recognize and appreciate in each other.
- ➤ Keep the recognition on par with the reward. If someone does something truly outstanding, perhaps something more than a candy bar is appropriate.
- ➤ Don't worry about everyone getting a candy bar. This is not about fairness. (Maybe those who do not get one this time will think about why they did not get recognized, and change.) This is especially OK if you make this activity a regular or semiregular activity for the group.
- ➤ If someone gives a candy bar and is not specific, ask them to share an example (not to "test" them, but to give the rest of the group an idea of what specifically is being recognized).

Try these variations . . .

- ➤ You can use other small rewards besides Kudos® bars—perhaps something more relevant to your organization?
- ➤ Give a candy bar to each participant, and have each give it to someone else in recognition or appreciation.

LABELS

This is . . . A planning activity in which participants treat each other differently based on written labels they wear on their foreheads.

The purpose is . . . Participants learn first hand how it feels to be treated a certain way because of generalizations or prejudices. They learn how this hampers good communication.

Use this when . . .
- ➤ The group needs to appreciate the diversity of its members better.
- ➤ Individuals are approaching each other, customers, partners, or others with preconceived notions about them.
- ➤ Labels and prejudices are getting in the way of communication and collaboration.

Materials you'll need . . .
- ➤ A set of six labels for each group. Labels should be large enough that participants can read them from several feet away.
- ➤ Labels can be directive, like "disagree with me," "ignore me," "treat me like the leader," "laugh at me," "respect my opinions," "find fault with me," "argue with me," "agree with me," "interrupt me," and so forth. Or, they can be simple labels, such as "arrogant," "helpful," "self-promoting," "brown-noser," "cooperative," "a pushover," "defensive," "leader," and so forth.

Here's **how . . .**	1. Divide the group into teams of six.
	2. Distribute a set of six labels to each team, face down.
	3. Each team member sticks a label on the forehead of the person next to him or her.
	4. All participants can read what is on others' labels but not their own. Do not tell anyone what is on his or her own label.
	5. Give the teams a task to plan (plan a departmental picnic, how they will participate in this year's community fund raiser, etc.). They will have 7 minutes to do this.
	6. As they discuss, they must respect the label each participant is wearing. React and respond according to what it says.
	7. After 7 minutes, even if the task is not complete, stop the teams and discuss.

Ask these
questions . . .

➤ What happened? Did you accomplish your task? Why or why not?

➤ How satisfied are you with the outcome? Why?

➤ How did you feel about treating people with these labels? *(It was not me; It felt forced; It was fun; etc.)* Did it get easier over time? Why? *(Others reinforced the label; I got used to treating her that way; etc.)*

➤ How did you feel about the way you were being treated? *(Frustrated, angry, puzzled, annoyed, etc.)* What was your reaction then? *(I fought harder; I disengaged; I treated him even worse; etc.)*

➤ What implications does this have for us back on the job?

Tips for
success . . .

➤ Use your judgment in dividing teams. For example, if you have 11 participants, remove one label from one set, and have one team of 6 and one team of 5 participants, so that everyone can have the experience. If there are 13 participants, have a seventh label ready.

➤ Some people may be reluctant to adhere to the labels. As you observe, encourage participants to take the labels they see to heart and act accordingly.

Try these
variations . . .

➤ Try different labels or different combinations of labels with different teams to explore various themes or dynamics.

➤ Precede this activity with an activity to reinforce creativity and individuality. Have each participant make a paper hat from newsprint. Then affix the labels to their hats and have them wear them for this activity.

➤ Make the labels represent different stakeholders on a project or different types of customers and so forth.

➤ Have only one group of six to eight participants with labels do the task, while the rest of your group observes.

➤ Instead of planning a picnic, have the teams grapple with a real work-related problem or issue.

RAINBOW OF DIVERSITY

This is . . .	An activity in which participants use crayons as a metaphor for their own diversity.
The purpose is . . .	Participants appreciate the similarities and differences among themselves.
Use this when . . .	➤ Individuals need to recognize and appreciate what's going *right* among them.
	➤ Individuals are not appreciating each other very well.
	➤ Individuals need to bond together
Materials you'll need . . .	➤ A different colored crayon for each participant (for a large group, get a large box of 64 crayons!).
Here's how . . .	1. Give a crayon to each participant.
	2. Have them pair up with someone else whose crayon color is close to their own color.
	3. They have 2 minutes to discover all the ways that they, as individuals, are similar to each other.
	4. Have them pair up again, this time with someone whose crayon color is very different from their own color.
	5. They now have 2 minutes to discover all the ways that they, as individuals, are different from each other.

6. Have the participants get in a circle, standing next to colors that are most like their own. This will make a sort of round rainbow. Conduct the Debrief while they are in this circle.

Ask these questions . . .

➤ What did you learn about the participant with a color similar to yours?
➤ What did you learn about the participant with a color different from yours?
➤ What does this circle say about our team? (*Even though I am standing next to someone similar, I am ultimately connected to the very different person opposite me in the circle; We are one big whole; etc*)
➤ What implications does this have for us back on the job?

Tips for success . . .

➤ Do not let them get too worried about the "correct" closest color or opposite color. Yes, green is opposite red on the color wheel, but it is also quite different from black, silver, orange, pink, and many other colors.

Try these variations . . .

➤ Have the group make a colorful creation on a flipchart page. Make sure each participant contributes his or her color. How is each color critical to the success of the whole? Does each color have to be used equally for the creation to be beautiful?
➤ When the participants pair up with a color close to theirs, have them point out what strengths they have in common that contribute to the success of the group. When they pair up with a different color, have them identify what each other's strengths are and how they can learn from or appreciate those different skills and abilities.

WHAT I LIKE ABOUT ME

This is . . .   A discussion activity in which participants tell each other what their own strengths are.

The purpose is . . .   Participants realize how much they have to offer, how valuable they are to the team, and that it's OK to acknowledge their own accomplishments.

Use this when . . .
- ➤ Individuals need a boost of self-esteem.
- ➤ Individuals are not feeling confident about their ability to get the job done.
- ➤ You don't have prep time and/or materials for anything more elaborate.

Materials you'll need . . .
- ➤ No materials are necessary for this activity.

Here's how . . .
1. Have the participants pair up.
2. One partner will talk to the other one for 3 minutes nonstop about what they have accomplished at work lately.
3. If the speaker says anything that diminishes or minimizes their accomplishment, the listener will say, "I object." The speaker must then retract their comment.
4. Other than that, the listener may not speak at all.
5. After 3 minutes, reverse roles and repeat.

For example . . .

Speaker: "I did a good job on the XYZ account. When they called and asked me those tough questions, at first I was baffled. Then I asked Michael for help, and I felt more comfortable answering them. Of course, Michael probably could have handled it better without me, but at least I was able to. . ."

Listener: "I object!"

Speaker: "OK, scratch that. I was able to answer their questions with Michael's help. Period. Let's see, another thing I did was. . ."

Ask these questions . . .

➤ Which role was easier for you, the listener or the speaker? Why? *(Most will say the listener.)*

➤ How did you feel about listening without being able to ask questions or contribute your own thoughts? *(Stifled, not part of the conversation, not sure I was understanding, bored, etc.)*

➤ How did you feel about speaking without being able to check in with your listener? *(Egotistical, not sure she was "with" me, unsure of myself, etc.)*

➤ What did you learn about how you feel about yourself? *(I need validation; I'm not comfortable acknowledging my own strengths; I put too much [or too little] emphasis on what others think of me; etc.)*

➤ How do you think this affects how you do your job?

Tips for success . . .

➤ The hardest thing for the speakers will be talking continuously. They may hesitate to acknowledge their contributions. This may come out as they pause to "think of something good." Encourage the speakers to just keep talking. If they run out of things to talk about, tell them to go back in time and keep going back, even if they end up talking about things they did 15 years ago. The point is to realize and acknowledge their own

value and contributions without editing or
censoring.

➤ Add competitiveness. The listener gets 1 point every
time the speaker pauses for more than 5 seconds
and 5 points every time the listener catches them
with an "I object." Be prepared with small prizes
for the winner. Ask later if the competitive pressure impacted the speaker.

➤ Limit the speakers' monologues to a specific project they have worked on recently as a team. This
will help them highlight the diverse and important contributions each has made to the success
of the team.

➤ Limit the speakers' monologues to a specific orga-
nizational value or core competency. This will
help them reinforce those appropriate behaviors
in themselves and in each other.

➤ Have the participants answer the discussion questions in their pairs, rather than in the larger group.

Z, Y, X, W, V... ZYX

This is . . . A verbal activity in which the participants learn to say the alphabet backwards as quickly as they can say it forwards.

The purpose is . . . Participants realize they have different learning styles, and they should take advantage of their preferred style when they learn new skills at work. This activity also builds confidence.

Use this when . . .
- ➤ Individuals are facing a steep learning curve.
- ➤ The group lacks confidence to accomplish what is ahead of them.
- ➤ You don't have prep time and/or materials for anything more elaborate.

Materials you'll need . . .
- ➤ No materials are necessary for this activity.

Here's how . . .
1. Ask the group to recite the alphabet with you. Do this at a decent speed, but do not rush through it.
2. Tell them that the objective is to be able to recite (which means no reading) the alphabet backwards as quickly as they just did it forwards.
3. Participants may use any resources available in the room (paper, each other, you, etc.) to get ready.
4. They have 12 minutes to prepare and practice.
5. Lead the group in reciting the alphabet backwards at the same speed as you did forwards.

For example . . .	Z, Y, X, W, V, U, T, S, R, Q, P, O, N, M, L, K, J, I, H, G, F, E, D, C, B, A.
Ask these questions . . .	➤ How did you feel when you first heard the objective? *(This is impossible; This is silly; I can't do it; etc.)*
	➤ What strategy helped you prepare the most? (Look for indications of different learning styles.) Did you find you had to break the task into smaller pieces?
	➤ Did you offer or seek help from others trying to learn the same skill? Why or why not?
	➤ What other creative ways could we have used to help us learn together better?
	➤ What implications does this have for us back on the job?
Tips for success . . .	➤ People have different ways of learning: some are visual (by seeing), some are auditory (by saying or singing), and others are kinesthetic (by moving) learners. Visual learners will do best to write the alphabet backwards and look at it over and over. Auditory learner will do best by trying to say, sing, or just read the alphabet over and over. Kinesthetic learners will do best by pacing, doodling, or otherwise moving while they rehearse. Watch for indications of which style is adopted successfully by whom.
	➤ If you elect to have participants recite individually, be open to creative solutions. For example, when it is Karen's turn to recite, she may have a partner whisper the alphabet backwards in her ear as she repeats what she hears aloud!
Try these variations . . .	➤ For more competitive groups, have them individually recite the alphabet backwards. You may even want to time them. If the group is larger than six

to eight people, divide them into smaller groups for the final, individual reciting.

➤ Use the Pledge of Allegiance instead of the alphabet or (if it is short enough) your organization's mission statement.

INDEX

ABOUT THE AUTHOR

Brian Cole Miller is the founder of Working Solutions (Columbus, Ohio), which specializes in building more confident and competent Front Line Leaders (www.WorkingSolutionsOnline.com). He has provided training, coaching, and consulting to clients that include Nationwide Insurance, Franklin Covey, Anthem Blue Cross Blue Shield, and UPS.